Weight Watchers®

Slim Ways™

ITALIAN

Macmillan • USA

Weight Watchers

Since 1963, Weight Watchers has grown from a handful of people to millions of enrollments annually. Today, Weight Watchers is the recognized leading name in safe, sensible weight control. Weight Watchers members form a diverse group, from youths to senior citizens, attending meetings virtually around the globe.

Weight-loss and weight-management results vary by individual, but we recommend that you attend Weight Watchers meetings, follow the Weight Watchers food plan and participate in regular physical activity. For the Weight Watchers meeting nearest you, call 1-800-651-6000.

Thanks to everyone who helped put this cookbook together: recipe developers Barbara Posner Beltrami and Linda Romanelli Leahy; nutrition consultants Lynne S. Hill, M.S., R.D., L.D., and William Hill, M.S., R.D., L.D.

Senior Editor: Martha Schueneman
Cover photo by Martin Jacobs
Cover photo: Farfalle with Grilled Swordfish and Vegetables, p. 64

MACMILLAN
A Simon & Schuster Macmillan Company
1633 Broadway
New York, NY 10019-6785

Library of Congress Cataloging-in-Publication Data
Weight watchers slim ways : Italian / [Weight Watchers editors].
      p.   cm.
    Includes index.
    ISBN 0-02-861498-4 (alk. paper)
    1. Reducing diets—Recipes: 2. Cookery, Italian.   I. Weight
Watchers International.
  RM222.2.W3278   1997
  641.5'635—dc21   96-46918
                                                        CIP

Manufactured in the United States of America
10   9   8   7   6   5   4   3   2   1

CONTENTS

How to Convert Recipes to the Freedom Plan

All the recipes in *Slim Ways Italian* are adaptable for the Weight Watchers Freedom Plan. All you have to do is change the Selection™ Information to fit the Freedom Plan. Here's how you do it:

Breads don't change at all.
Bread Selection = 1 Bread

Add the Protein and Milk Selections together to come up with the number of Protein/Milks
1 Milk Selection = 1 Protein/Milk
1 Protein Selection = 1 Protein/Milk

Fruits don't change at all, but 2 Vegetable Selections are now 1 Fruit/Vegetables. Add the Fruit and Vegetable Selections together to come up with the total number of Fruit/Vegetables.
1 Fruit Selection = 1 Fruit/Vegetable
2 Vegetable Selections = 1 Fruit/Vegetable

Fats don't change at all.
1 Fat Selection = 1 Fat

Round any fractions up or down.

INTRODUCTION

In recent years, authentic Italian cuisine has exploded in popularity—and it's easy to understand why. While many of us associate heavy meat sauces and overstuffed hero sandwiches with Italian cuisine, true Italian food is based on flavorsome yet healthful ingredients, and has a light, fresh touch to it. Cooks in Italy rely on foods harvested at their peak of flavor, whether it's fish and seafood from the Mediterranean or vegetables and herbs from their gardens. Such authentic ingredients benefit most from simple preparations, and when accented with fruity olive oils, tangy wine vinegars and sharp Parmesan cheese, result in dishes with real flair.

Weight Watchers Slim Ways Italian shares 150 recipes, tested in home kitchens, for everything from antipasti to desserts. Here are healthful versions of all your favorite dishes, including lower-in-fat and lower-in-calorie versions of Fettuccine Alfredo and Tiramisu.

Most of the ingredients and cooking terms used in this book are commonplace, but here are a few that may be less familiar.

Al dente (ahl-DEN-tay): This Italian phrase means "to the tooth." It's used to describe foods, primarily pastas, that are cooked just until they are tender—offering gentle resistance "to the tooth" when bitten—but not soft.
Amaretti: Amaretti are crispy macaroon cookies flavored with a bitter-almond or apricot-kernel paste.

Anchovy: Similar to the sardine and herring, the anchovy is popular in southern European cuisine. These tiny fish are usually sold in tins (anchovies are very salty, so rinse them thoroughly before using). Anchovy paste (a mixture of mashed anchovies, vinegar, water and spices) is easier to use than canned fish and can be stored indefinitely in the refrigerator.

Antipasto: Literally translated "before the pasta," this term refers to appetizers: stuffed vegetables and clams are popular, as are bruschetta and crostini. Mixed antipasti plates are usually a combination of smoked or cured meats, cheeses, marinated vegetables, olives and fish, garnished with hard-cooked eggs and shavings of Parmesan cheese.

Arborio rice (ahr-BOH-ree-oh): Arborio is a short-grain rice with a high starch content that makes it creamy when cooked. It can be found in gourmet grocery stores and some supermarkets.

Arugula (ah-ROO-guh-luh): Arugula is a flavorsome, somewhat bitter salad green that's very popular in Italy. It can be used on its own or tossed into a salad with other greens. It can be found in specialty produce markets and some supermarkets.

Balsamic Vinegar: Made only in Italy, this smooth yet pungent vinegar is aged over a period of several years in wooden barrels to give it a dark color and sweetish flavor.

Biscotti: These Italian cookies are baked twice: first as a loaf, which is then sliced; the slices are then rebaked until very crisp.

Broccoli Rabe or **Rape**: Broccoli rabe is a pungent, bitter green that's not as popular in America as in Italy, where it's often sauteed, braised or steamed, as well as used in soups and salads. It is available in many markets from fall to early spring.

Bruschetta (broo-SKEH-tuh; broo-SHEH-tuh): This garlic bread is traditionally made by grilling slices of hearty peasant bread over hot coals, then rubbing it with the cut side of a garlic clove and drizzling extra-virgin olive oil over it.

Capers: These flower buds are used as a seasoning or condiment. Because they're most often packed in vinegar or salt, they should be rinsed before using.

Cappelletti: Similar to ravioli, cappelletti ("little caps") are small stuffed squares of pasta.

Crostini (kroh-STEE-nee): These "little toasts" are thin slices of Italian bread that are toasted, sometimes brushed with olive oil, and topped with cheese, tomatoes, seafood or other savory toppings.

Espresso (ehs-PREHS-oh): This coffee, made from the darkly roasted, finely ground beans of the same name, is brewed in a special pot or urn. Hot water or steam is forced through the grounds, which leaves a thin coating of froth on the surface of the drink. It is usually served black after a meal.

Fennel: Although its flavor is often compared to that of licorice, fennel's flavor is much subtler—it's also one of the most characteristic flavors in Italian cooking. This vegetable's bulbous base is delicious baked, braised, sauteed, or slivered raw into salads. Fennel is available from fall through spring in most supermarkets.

Focaccia (foh-KAH-chee-ah): Focaccia is a yeast-risen bread that's shaped into a large flat rectangle, drizzled with olive oil and sprinkled with seasonings—often salt or rosemary—before it's baked. Enjoy it as a snack, as a sandwich bread or serve it with soup or a salad.

Frittata: An Italian omelet that's prepared open-face, with the "fillings" sprinkled on top rather than folded in.

Gnocchi (NYOH-kee): Italian for "dumplings," gnocchi are small round pasta made from a dough of mashed potatoes.

Grappa (GRAH-pah): Grappa is a sharp, dry Italian brandy with a high alcohol content that's distilled from marc—the grape skins and seeds left in the wine press after the juice has been removed for wine.

Gremolada (greh-moh-LAH-tah): This garnish, made of minced parsley, lemon zest and garlic, imparts a fresh flavor to osso buco and other dishes.

Italian Frying Peppers: Pale green and cone-shaped, these sweet peppers are almost always served stuffed or sauteed.

Marsala: Marsala is a fortified Sicilian wine that is available both sweet and dry. Most imported Marsala is sweet, and is served as a dessert wine or used to flavor desserts and savory meat dishes. Dry Marsala is usually served as an apéritif.

Pasta Machines: Pasta machines fall into one of two categories. Extruder pasta machines, similar to bread machines, mix the dough inside the machine and then force it through plates with holes of various shapes and sizes. Roller-type pasta machines (available in hand-cranked or electric models), require that you mix the dough by hand or in a food processor before passing it between smooth rollers (creating sheets of the desired thickness) and then feeding it through notched rollers, which cut the sheets into noodles.

Pine nuts: These cream-colored—and creamy textured—nuts are from a variety of pine tree that grows in southern Europe and the southwestern

United States. They are used to flavor sweet and savory dishes, but are perhaps best known as an ingredient in pesto. Pine nuts can be found in many supermarkets and health food stores. Because they are very high in fat, they can become rancid very quickly and should be stored in the refrigerator or freezer.

Polenta: Polenta, a mush made from a coarse yellow cornmeal, is available in regular or instant (quick-cooking) varieties in gourmet grocery stores and some supermarkets.

Prosciutto (proh-SHOO-toh): Most accurately referred to as "prosciutto di Parma," this dry-cured Italian ham is sold in very thin slices in gourmet and Italian markets and some supermarkets. Because extended cooking can toughen it, it's best served as is—it is particularly delicious with melon or figs—or added at the last minute to pasta sauces or vegetable dishes.

Radicchio (rah-DEE-kee-oh): This slightly bitter, red-leafed chicory is often used as a salad green, though it is also delicious braised, baked, sauteed or grilled. It is available year round, but it is best from midwinter to early spring.

Risotto (ree-ZAW-toh): This Tuscan specialty is made by sauteing Arborio rice (frequently with chopped onions), then gradually adding small amounts of broth or another liquid until the rice is tender and the mixture is smooth and creamy. Because the rice needs to be stirred continually while the liquid is added, this meal is labor intensive.

Semolina (seh-moh-LEE-nuh): Semolina is a coarsely ground wheat flour used to make pastas and some breads.

Swiss Chard: A type of beet grown for its leaves rather than its roots. The stalks, which can be white or red, can be used like celery or asparagus; the leaves are cooked like spinach or cabbage.

Weight Watchers®

Slim Ways™

ITALIAN

1

BASICS

Fresh Pasta Dough

Meat-Filled Tortellini

Pumpkin-Filled Cappelletti

Cheese-Filled Ravioli

Greens-Filled Ravioli

Potato Gnocchi

Potato Gnocchi with Pumpkin Sauce

Basil Gnocchi

Polenta

Polenta Gnocchi alla Romana

Italian Flag Polenta

Oil and Vinegar Salad Dressing

Meat Sauce

Tomato Sauce

Tomato-Herb Sauce

FRESH PASTA DOUGH

Light and tender, this pasta can be used in just about any recipe. If you're using it for filled pasta, your yield will vary slightly, depending on the thinness and elasticity of the dough. Once rolled and cut, the pasta can be used fresh, dried or frozen.

Makes approximately 1 pound fresh pasta dough or 6–8 ounces dried pasta (enough for 4 dozen filled pastas).

$1^3/_4$ cups minus 1 tablespoon all-purpose flour

3 eggs, at room temperature
$^1/_4$ teaspoon salt

MANUAL METHOD:

1. Onto a clean, dry work surface, spoon approximately $1^1/_2$ cups of the flour into a mound. Make a well in the center of the flour; break the eggs into the well and add the salt. With a fork or small wire whisk, lightly beat the liquid ingredients into the well, gradually incorporating the flour. When the mixture becomes very thick and too difficult to mix, use your hands to scoop together any loose particles and form the dough into a ball; the dough should feel wet and sticky. Set the dough aside.

2. Scrape up the flour and any bits of dough that are stuck to the work surface. Transfer to a sieve; shake or tap out the usable flour and discard any dried or hard pieces of dough. Gradually add the sifted flour and the remaining 3 tablespoons flour to the dough, kneading it until smooth and satiny and no longer sticky, about 5–7 minutes.

3. Transfer the dough to a roller-type pasta machine and proceed according to the manufacturer's instructions.

FOOD PROCESSOR METHOD:

1. Fit the food processor with the plastic blade. Measure $1^1/_4$ cups of the flour into the work bowl. In a small bowl, lightly beat the eggs and salt with a fork or wire whisk; add to the flour. Pulse 4–5 times, until the dough is blended and crumbly, but does not yet hold together in a ball.

2. Turn the mixture onto a clean, dry work surface and knead the dough, gradually incorporating the remaining $^1/_4$ cup + 3 tablespoons flour, until the dough is smooth and satiny and no longer sticky.

3. Transfer the dough to a roller-type pasta machine and proceed according to the manufacturer's instructions.

TO DRY THE PASTA:

Dust the cut pasta lightly with flour and arrange on clean dry cotton towels spread on a flat surface, or drape it over the backs of chairs or drying racks. When dry, carefully transfer it to a large bowl or platter. Store, uncovered, in a cool dry place 2–3 days, in the refrigerator for up to 2–3 weeks or in sealed plastic bags and freeze up to 1 month.

TO COOK THE PASTA:

Bring 4 quarts of water to a full boil in a large pot. Add the pasta and stir; when the water returns to a boil, stir again and begin timing. Fresh pasta takes only 10–15 seconds to cook after the water returns to a boil; if it has been dried or frozen, it will take a few minutes longer. Test frequently for doneness. Drain the pasta; do not rinse with cold water.

Serving (4 ounces fresh pasta dough or 2 ounces dried) provides:
$^3/_4$ Protein, $2^1/_4$ Breads.

Per Serving: 248 Calories, 4 g Total Fat, 1 g Saturated Fat, 159 mg Cholesterol, 183 mg Sodium, 41 g Total Carbohydrate, 1 g Dietary Fiber, 10 g Protein, 27 mg Calcium.

MEAT-FILLED TORTELLINI

You can use this filling for tortellini, cappelletti or ravioli. Try it with different sauces or broths to enhance its delicate flavor and texture. However, try it at least once with the classic Tomato-Herb Sauce (page 21) and a light sprinkling of freshly grated Parmesan cheese. Since each piece of filled pasta requires only ¹/₂ teaspoon, a little goes a long way. Double or halve the recipe according to your needs and freeze any extra for later use.

Makes 4 servings

2 teaspoons reduced-calorie tub
 margarine
1 ounce ground skinless turkey
 breast
1 ounce ground skinless chicken
 breast
¹/₄ teaspoon ground white pepper
1 ounce high-quality bologna,
 chopped

¹/₄ cup part-skim ricotta cheese
³/₄ ounce Parmesan cheese, grated
1 egg white
¹/₄ teaspoon ground nutmeg
1 teaspoon all-purpose flour
1 pound Fresh Pasta Dough
 (page 2)

1. Place a large nonstick skillet over medium heat 30 seconds; melt the margarine 30 seconds more. Add the turkey, chicken and pepper and cook, stirring constantly to break up the meat, about 5 minutes, until the meat is no longer pink. With a slotted spoon, transfer to a cutting board. Add the bologna and, using a sharp knife, mince until very fine.
2. In a medium bowl, combine the meat mixture, ricotta, cheese, egg white and nutmeg; mix thoroughly. Cover and refrigerate until ready to use, up to 8 hours.
3. Lightly dust a clean dry work surface with the flour. Place a sheet of wax paper on a baking sheet and lightly spray with nonstick cooking spray; set aside.
4. Break off a chunk of pasta dough the size of a lemon; keep the remaining dough covered. Using a roller-type pasta machine, roll the dough as thin as possible into a roughly 18×6" rectangle. Transfer to the prepared work surface.
5. Using a 2¹/₂–3" round cookie or biscuit cutter or sharp-rimmed glass, cut the pasta into 12 disks. One at a time, place ¹/₂ teaspoon of filling in the center of each disk; fold the disk in half to form a semi-circle, then press down firmly to seal the edges. Holding it gently between your index finger and thumb

with curved edge up, wrap it around your index finger until the two points meet, then fold back the curved edge. Pinch the ends firmly to seal. As you finish each piece, place it on the prepared wax paper, making sure the tortellini don't touch. Repeat with the remaining dough (incorporate scraps into your next sheets or freeze for later use) and filling to make 48 tortellini. Refrigerate the tortellini, uncovered, until ready to use, up to 2 days, turning them occasionally to dry evenly, or freeze them first on the wax paper–lined baking sheet, then in sealable plastic bags up to 1 month. (They are easier to handle when frozen.) Do not thaw before cooking.

6. Into a large pot of boiling water, gently drop the tortellini, a few at a time, to avoid tearing them; if fresh, make sure they don't stick to each other. Cook 7–8 minutes, until tender. With a slotted spoon, transfer the tortellini to a warm serving bowl. Add the sauce of your choice and toss gently to coat. Divide evenly among 4 plates and serve.

Serving (12 tortellini) provides: $^1/_4$ Fat, $1^3/_4$ Proteins, $2^1/_4$ Breads, 10 Optional Calories.

Per Serving: 351 Calories, 11 g Total Fat, 4 g Saturated Fat, 181 mg Cholesterol, 410 mg Sodium, 43 g Total Carbohydrate, 1 g Dietary Fiber, 19 g Protein, 146 mg Calcium.

PUMPKIN-FILLED CAPPELLETTI

Pumpkin purée makes this pasta stuffing easy; make a double or even triple batch of cappelletti and freeze the filled pasta for holiday dinners. For a simple yet delicious sauce, melt reduced-calorie tub margarine with some crumbled fresh or dried sage. The herb's slightly bitter flavor provides a perfect foil for the sweet filling.

Makes 4 servings

$^1/_2$ cup pumpkin purée
1 tablespoon part-skim ricotta
  cheese
$^3/_4$ ounce Parmesan cheese, grated
$^1/_2$ amaretti cookie (1" diameter),
  crushed into fine crumbs

$^1/_4$ teaspoon salt
$^1/_4$ teaspoon ground white pepper
$^1/_8$ teaspoon ground nutmeg
1 teaspoon all-purpose flour
1 pound Fresh Pasta Dough
  (page 2)

1. In a medium bowl, combine the pumpkin purée, ricotta and Parmesan cheeses and cookie crumbs. Season with salt, pepper and nutmeg.
2. Lightly dust a clean dry surface with the flour. Place a sheet of wax paper on a baking sheet and lightly spray with nonstick cooking spray; set aside.
3. Break off a chunk of pasta dough the size of a lemon; keep the remaining dough covered. Using a roller-type pasta machine, roll the dough as thin as possible. Transfer to the prepared surface and trim to form an 18×6" rectangle.
4. With a sharp knife or pastry cutter, cut the dough into 3" squares. One at a time, place half-teaspoons of the filling in the center of each square; fold over to make a triangle. Seal the edges and fold back peaked edge. Holding gently between your index finger and thumb with the point up, wrap around your index finger and press together lightly to seal. As you finish each piece, place on the prepared wax paper, making sure that the cappelletti don't touch. Repeat with the remaining dough (incorporate scraps into your next sheets) and filling to make 48 cappelletti. Refrigerate the cappelletti, uncovered, until ready to use, for up to 8 hours, or freeze first on the wax paper–lined baking sheet, then in sealable plastic bags up to 1 month. (They are easier to handle when frozen.) Do not thaw before cooking.

5. Into a large pot of boiling water, gently drop the cappelletti, a few at a time, to avoid tearing them; if fresh, make sure they don't stick to each other. Cook 7–8 minutes, until tender. With a slotted spoon, transfer to a warm serving bowl. Add the sauce of your choice and toss gently to coat. Divide evenly among 4 plates and serve.

Serving (12 cappelletti) provides: $1/4$ Vegetable, 1 Protein, $2^{1}/_{4}$ Breads, 15 Optional Calories.

Per Serving: 290 Calories, 6 g Total Fat, 2 g Saturated Fat, 165 mg Cholesterol, 423 mg Sodium, 44 g Total Carbohydrate, 1 g Dietary Fiber, 13 g Protein, 117 mg Calcium.

Cheese-Filled Ravioli

Cheese filling freezes well, so make a double batch and stuff manicotti or other pastas for another meal. This ravioli tastes best with a light and fairly smooth fresh tomato sauce.

Makes 4 servings

$^1/_2$ cup part-skim ricotta cheese	$^1/_4$ teaspoon ground white pepper
$^3/_4$ ounce Parmesan cheese, grated	$^1/_8$ teaspoon ground nutmeg
2 tablespoons minced fresh flat-leaf parsley	1 teaspoon all-purpose flour
$^1/_2$ egg white	1 pound Fresh Pasta Dough (page 2)

1. In a medium bowl, combine the ricotta and Parmesan cheeses, parsley, egg white, pepper and nutmeg.
2. Lightly dust a clean dry surface with the flour. Place a sheet of wax paper on a baking sheet and lightly spray with nonstick cooking spray; set aside.
3. Break off a chunk of pasta dough the size of a lemon; keep the remaining dough covered. Using a roller-type pasta machine, roll the dough as thin as possible. Transfer to the prepared surface and trim to form a 17×6" rectangle.
4. Starting 1" from the top and side edges, place half-teaspoons of filling 2" apart on the sheet.
5. Break off another lemon-size chunk of dough, incorporating the scraps from the first sheet. Roll another sheet of dough as thin as possible and trim to form another 17×6" rectangle. Gently place over first layer to cover the filling.
6. To seal the edges, making sure the filling will be in the center of each ravioli, with a moistened finger, draw lines between the dots of filling, first lengthwise, then crosswise. With a pastry cutter, trace the lines and cut into twenty-four 2" squares. With the tip of a knife, carefully lift and transfer the squares to the prepared wax paper, making sure the ravioli don't touch. Repeat with the remaining dough (incorporate scraps into your next sheets or freeze for later use) and filling to make 48 ravioli. Refrigerate the ravioli, uncovered, until ready to use, up to 2 hours,* or freeze first on the wax paper–lined baking sheet, then in sealable plastic bags up to 1 month. (They are easier to handle when frozen.) Do not thaw before cooking.

7. Into a large pot of boiling water, gently drop the ravioli, a few at a time, to avoid tearing them; if fresh, make sure they don't stick to each other. Cook 7–8 minutes, until tender. With a slotted spoon, transfer the ravioli to a warm serving bowl. Add the sauce of your choice, and toss gently to coat. Divide evenly among 4 plates and serve.

Serving (12 ravioli) provides: $1^1/_2$ Proteins, $2^1/_4$ Breads, 5 Optional Calories.

Per Serving: 320 Calories, 8 g Total Fat, 4 g Saturated Fat, 173 mg Cholesterol, 328 mg Sodium, 43 g Total Carbohydrate, 2 g Dietary Fiber, 16 g Protein, 187 mg Calcium.

This filling does not keep well in the refrigerator, so plan either to use it the same day you make it or to freeze it. Thaw in the refrigerator and use within 1–2 hours of thawing.

GREENS-FILLED RAVIOLI

Swiss chard and spinach, accented with a bit of onion and creamy ricotta cheese, make a healthful and delicious pasta filling. Any that is left over can be refrigerated for up to 2 days or frozen for later use. Although nothing beats a simple tomato sauce to enhance the flavor of this filling, Walnut Sauce (page 52) complements it very well too.

Makes 4 servings

1 cup well-washed trimmed Swiss chard

1 cup well-washed trimmed spinach

2 teaspoons reduced-calorie tub margarine

1/2 ounce well-trimmed prosciutto, finely chopped

2 tablespoons minced onion

1/4 cup part-skim ricotta cheese

3/4 ounce Parmesan cheese, grated

1 egg white, lightly beaten

1/4 teaspoon ground nutmeg

1/4 teaspoon freshly ground white pepper

1 teaspoon all-purpose flour

1 pound Fresh Pasta Dough (page 2)

1. In a large pot, bring 2" water to a boil. Arrange the Swiss chard and spinach on a steamer rack; place in the pot and cover with a tight-fitting lid. Steam 10 minutes, until tender. Drain; squeeze out excess moisture. Set aside in colander.

2. Place a medium nonstick skillet over medium heat 30 seconds; melt the margarine 30 seconds more. Add the prosciutto and onion; cook, stirring constantly, 2 minutes, until the onion is softened.

3. Squeeze the greens again to be sure no moisture remains; chop them very finely. Add them to the onion mixture; reduce the heat to low; cook, stirring constantly, 1 minute, until thoroughly coated with margarine. Transfer to a medium bowl. Add the ricotta and Parmesan cheeses, egg white, nutmeg and pepper; combine thoroughly.

4. Lightly dust a clean dry surface with the flour. Place a sheet of wax paper on a baking sheet; spray lightly with nonstick cooking spray and set aside.

5. Break off a chunk of pasta dough the size of a lemon; keep the remaining dough covered. Using a roller-type pasta machine, roll the dough as thin as possible. Transfer to the prepared surface and trim to form a 17×6" rectangle.

6. Starting 1" from the top and side edges, place half-teaspoons of filling 2" apart on sheet.

7. Break off another lemon-size chunk of dough; incorporating the scraps from the first sheet, roll another sheet of dough as thin as possible and trim to form another 17×6" rectangle. Gently place over the first sheet to cover the filling.

8. To seal the edges, making sure the filling will be in the center of each ravioli, with a moistened finger draw lines between the dots of filling, first lengthwise, then crosswise. With a pastry cutter, trace the lines and cut into twenty-four 2" squares. With the tip of a knife, carefully lift and transfer the squares to the prepared wax paper, making sure the ravioli do not touch. Repeat with the remaining dough (incorporate scraps into your next sheets or freeze for later use) and filling to make 48 ravioli. Refrigerate the ravioli, uncovered, until ready to use, up to 2 days, or freeze first on the wax paper–lined baking sheet, then in sealable plastic bags up to 1 month. (They are easier to handle when frozen.) Do not thaw before cooking.

9. Into a large pot of boiling water, gently drop the ravioli, a few at a time, to avoid tearing them; if fresh, make sure they don't stick to each other. Cook 7–8 minutes, until tender. With a slotted spoon, carefully transfer to a warm serving bowl. Add the sauce of your choice and toss gently to coat. Divide evenly among 4 plates and serve.

Serving (12 ravioli) provides: $1/4$ Fat, 1 Vegetable, $1^1/4$ Proteins, $2^1/4$ Breads, 15 Optional Calories.

Per Serving: 328 Calories, 9 g Total Fat, 3 g Saturated Fat, 171 mg Cholesterol, 425 mg Sodium, 44 g Total Carbohydrate, 2 g Dietary Fiber, 17 g Protein, 163 mg Calcium.

POTATO GNOCCHI

These feather-weight potato dumplings are great with any light, not-too-chunky sauce. Try them with Tomato Sauce (page 20), Tomato-Herb Sauce (page 21) or Basil Pesto (page 142), as well as with Pumpkin Sauce (page 13).

Makes 4 servings (or 72 gnocchi)

15 ounces baking potatoes, scrubbed

$^1/_2$ cup + 2 tablespoons all-purpose flour

$^1/_4$ teaspoon salt

1. Preheat the oven to 400° F. With a sharp knife, cut an X into each potato. Bake 1 hour, until tender in the center when pierced with a knife. Set the potatoes aside 10 minutes, until cool enough to handle.
2. Peel the potatoes and discard the skins. Press the pulp through a ricer or food mill into a large bowl; there should be about $1^1/_2$ cups potato pulp.
3. While the pulp is still hot, stir in $^1/_2$ cup of the flour and the salt. Sprinkle a clean dry work surface with the remaining 2 tablespoons flour; turn out the potato mixture and knead until smooth but slightly sticky. Break off a chunk of dough the size of a lemon; keep the remaining dough covered.
4. Roll the pasta dough into a 1" thick cylinder. With a sharp knife, cut into 1" lengths. Roll each cut piece against the tines of a dinner fork to make decorative grooves; set aside on wax paper, making sure the gnocchi don't touch. Breaking off only one piece at a time and keeping the remaining dough covered, repeat the procedure until all the dough is used. Refrigerate, lightly covered, up to 2 days or freeze first on trays, then in sealable plastic bags up to 1 month.
5. In a large pot of boiling water, cook the gnocchi in batches without crowding, about 30–45 seconds, until they float to the surface. With a slotted spoon, transfer to a serving bowl. Toss lightly with the sauce of your choice. Repeat until all gnocchi are cooked. Divide evenly among 4 plates and serve.

Serving (about 18 gnocchi) provides: $1^1/_2$ Breads, 10 Optional Calories.

Per Serving: 150 Calories, 0 g Total Fat, 0 g Saturated Fat, 0 mg Cholesterol, 140 mg Sodium, 33 g Total Carbohydrate, 2 g Dietary Fiber, 4 g Protein, 8 mg Calcium.

POTATO GNOCCHI WITH PUMPKIN SAUCE

With its intriguing sauce, this dish is a favorite in Lombardy and the Veneto. Refrigerate or freeze any extra sauce for another meal.

Makes 4 servings

1 tablespoon + 1 teaspoon olive oil
One 2-pound pumpkin, pared, halved, seeded and diced
3 shallots, minced
1 garlic clove, minced
2 cups low-sodium chicken broth
1 tablespoon minced fresh thyme leaves (or 1 teaspoon dried leaves, crumbled)
1 tablespoon minced fresh sage leaves (or 1 teaspoon dried leaves, crumbled)

$^1/_4$ teaspoon ground white pepper
72 Potato Gnocchi (page 12), hot
1 tablespoon + 1 teaspoon freshly grated Parmesan cheese
1 tablespoon firmly packed light or dark brown sugar
$^1/_4$ teaspoon cinnamon
$^1/_4$ teaspoon ground nutmeg
Fresh sage leaves, to garnish (optional)

1. Place a large nonstick skillet over medium heat 30 seconds; heat the oil 30 seconds more. Add the pumpkin, shallots and garlic; cook, stirring constantly, 3–5 minutes, until the shallots begin to turn golden. Add the broth, thyme, sage and pepper; cook, stirring frequently, 15–20 minutes more, until the pumpkin is softened and the liquid is reduced by two-thirds.
2. In a food processor or blender, purée the pumpkin mixture until smooth. If it is too thick, add 1 tablespoon water at a time until the mixture reaches the desired consistency.
3. Pour the sauce over the hot gnocchi; sprinkle evenly with the cheese, sugar, cinnamon and nutmeg. Serve garnished with sage leaves.

Serving (about 18 gnocchi with $^1/_3$ cup sauce) provides: 1 Fat, 1 Vegetable, $1^1/_2$ Breads, 40 Optional Calories.

Per Serving: 276 Calories, 7 g Total Fat, 1 g Saturated Fat, 1 mg Cholesterol, 233 mg Sodium, 50 g Total Carbohydrate, 2 g Dietary Fiber, 8 g Protein, 93 mg Calcium.

BASIL GNOCCHI

Italian for dumplings, gnocchi are made from potatoes. Although this might look like a lengthy recipe, these tender little morsels are easy—and fun—to make.

Makes 4 servings

15 ounces baking potatoes, scrubbed
1 cup minus 1 tablespoon all-purpose flour
$^1/_3$ cup + 2 teaspoons minced fresh basil

$^1/_4$ teaspoon salt
2 cups hot Tomato-Herb Sauce (page 21)
1 tablespoon + 1 teaspoon freshly grated Parmesan cheese

1. Preheat the oven to 400° F. With a sharp knife, cut an X into each potato. Bake 1 hour, until tender in the center when pierced with a knife.
2. Peel the potatoes and discard the skins. Press the pulp through a ricer or food mill into a large bowl.
3. While the pulp is still hot, stir in $^3/_4$ cup of the flour, $^1/_4$ cup of the basil and the salt. Sprinkle a clean dry work surface with the remaining 3 tablespoons flour; turn out the potato mixture and knead until smooth but slightly sticky. Break off a chunk of dough the size of a lemon; return the remaining dough to the bowl and cover.
4. Roll the pasta into a 1" thick cylinder. With a sharp knife, cut into 1" lengths. Roll each cut piece against the tines of a dinner fork to make decorative grooves; set aside on wax paper, making sure the gnocchi don't touch. Breaking off only one piece of dough at a time and keeping the remaining dough covered, repeat the procedure until all the dough is used.
5. Place $^1/_4$ cup Tomato-Herb Sauce in a large serving bowl.
6. In a large pot of boiling water, cook the gnocchi in batches without crowding, 30–45 seconds, until they float to the surface. With a slotted spoon, transfer immediately to the serving bowl in layers, alternating layers of sauce and gnocchi. Sprinkle with the remaining 2 tablespoons of basil and the cheese. Divide evenly among 4 plates and serve at once.

Serving (about 18 gnocchi with $^1/_2$ cup sauce) provides: 1 Fat, $1^1/_2$ Vegetables, 2 Breads, 10 Optional Calories.

Per Serving: 272 Calories, 6 g Total Fat, 1 g Saturated Fat, 2 mg Cholesterol, 327 mg Sodium, 49 g Total Carbohydrate, 4 g Dietary Fiber, 7 g Protein, 102 mg Calcium.

POLENTA

Although some people would call this just a simple cornmeal mush, polenta is every bit as important in northern Italy as pasta, rice and potatoes are elsewhere. It makes an excellent base for cheese and other delicious additions.

Makes 4 servings

$^1/_4$ teaspoon salt
1 cup coarse-ground yellow
   cornmeal

1. In a large heavy pot, bring $3^1/_2$ cups water to boil over high heat. Add the salt; reduce the heat so the water is barely simmering. Stirring constantly, slowly add the cornmeal in a very thin stream. Reduce the heat to low; cook, stirring constantly, 10–15 minutes, until the mixture pulls away from the sides of the pot.
2. If serving immediately, pour the polenta onto a large warm platter. If using in further preparation, pour onto a large wooden block or cutting board and allow to cool slightly before slicing.

Serving ($^3/_4$ cup) provides: 2 Breads.

Per Serving: 126 Calories, 1 g Total Fat, 0 g Saturated Fat, 0 mg Cholesterol, 136 mg Sodium, 27 g Total Carbohydrate, 2 g Dietary Fiber, 3 g Protein, 3 mg Calcium.

POLENTA GNOCCHI ALLA ROMANA

POLENTA GNOCCHI BAKED WITH CHEESE

Gnocchi alla Romana, traditionally made with semolina, is such a classic that it can be traced back to the ancient Romans. Substituting polenta makes this version less labor-intensive; the resulting dish is even more golden and glorious than the original!

Makes 4 servings

3 cups Polenta (page 15)
1¹/₂ ounces Parmesan cheese, grated

1 tablespoon + 1 teaspoon reduced-calorie tub margarine

1. Preheat the oven to 350° F. Spray a 9" pie pan with nonstick cooking spray.
2. Prepare Polenta through Step 1; turn onto a large wooden board. With a knife or spatula dipped in cold water, spread evenly to ¹/₄" thickness. Dip a 2" sharp-rimmed glass or biscuit cutter into cold water; cut polenta into 16 disks, dipping glass in cold water after each cut. Reserve scraps for another use.
3. Arrange the disks in the prepared pan, slightly overlapping as necessary; sprinkle evenly with the cheese and dot evenly with the margarine. Bake 40–50 minutes, until crisp and golden. Divide evenly among 4 plates and serve at once.

Serving (4 disks) provides: ¹/₂ Fat, ¹/₂ Protein, 2 Breads.

Per Serving: 200 Calories, 7 g Total Fat, 3 g Saturated Fat, 8 mg Cholesterol, 362 mg Sodium, 27 g Total Carbohydrate, 2 g Dietary Fiber, 7 g Protein, 149 mg Calcium.

ITALIAN FLAG POLENTA

Spinach, tomatoes and mozzarella, atop a polenta base, represent the colors of the Italian flag.

Makes 4 servings

3 cups Polenta (page 15)
4 cups thawed frozen chopped
   spinach (two 10-ounce packages)
2 cups Tomato Sauce (page 20)

3 ounces skim-milk mozzarella
   cheese, shredded
2 tablespoons + 2 teaspoons
   reduced-calorie tub margarine

1. Prepare the Polenta through Step 1; set aside.
2. Cook the spinach according to package directions; drain thoroughly and set aside.
3. Preheat the oven to 375° F. Spray a 13×9" baking dish with nonstick cooking spray. Spread 1 cup of the Tomato Sauce evenly over the bottom of the dish. Spread the Polenta in an even layer over the Tomato Sauce. Arrange the spinach evenly over the polenta; sprinkle the mozzarella evenly over the spinach. Top with the remaining 1 cup sauce; dot evenly with the margarine.
4. Bake the polenta about 20 minutes, until the cheese and sauce are bubbling. Cut into 4 equal pieces and serve.

Serving (¹/₄ of casserole) provides: 2 Fats, 3¹/₂ Vegetables, 1 Protein, 2 Breads.

Per Serving: 308 Calories, 11 g Total Fat, 2 g Saturated Fat, 2 mg Cholesterol, 603 mg Sodium, 40 g Total Carbohydrate, 7 g Dietary Fiber, 15 g Protein, 319 mg Calcium.

OIL AND VINEGAR SALAD DRESSING

This dressing is so light and fresh tasting that it perks up even the most ordinary green salad. Experiment by adding different herbs and spices, fruit juices, minced sun-dried tomatoes (not packed in oil) or olives, grated cheese and mustards.

Makes 4 servings

3 tablespoons dry white or red wine
1 tablespoon + 1 teaspoon olive oil
2 teaspoons balsamic vinegar
2 teaspoons white or red wine
vinegar
1 garlic clove, bruised

$^1/_4$ teaspoon dried oregano or
marjoram
$^1/_4$ teaspoon salt
Freshly ground black pepper, to
taste

In a small jar with a tight-fitting lid or a small bowl, combine the wine, oil, vinegars, garlic, oregano, salt and pepper; cover and shake well or, with wire whisk, blend until combined. Let stand at room temperature 20–30 minutes for flavors to blend; remove garlic before serving. If refrigerating, let come to room temperature before using.

Serving (1 tablespoon + 1 teaspoon) provides: 1 Fat, 10 Optional Calories.

Per Serving: 49 Calories, 4 g Total Fat, 1 g Saturated Fat, 0 mg Cholesterol, 136 mg Sodium, 1 g Total Carbohydrate, 0 g Dietary Fiber, 0 g Protein, 5 mg Calcium.

MEAT SAUCE

Best with a tubular pasta such as rigatoni and ziti or long thick strands such as tagliatelle and fettuccine, this sauce is a robust staple in any Italian kitchen. Serve it with a green salad or vegetable and, as they say in Italy, *Ecco!* You have a meal!

Makes 4 servings

1³/₄ cups canned whole Italian
    plum tomatoes (no salt added),
    with their juice
2 teaspoons olive oil
¹/₂ medium onion, chopped
1 medium celery stalk, minced
¹/₄ cup minced carrot
1 garlic clove, minced
4 ounces lean ground beef
    (10% or less fat)

¹/₄ teaspoon salt
¹/₄ teaspoon ground white pepper
2 fluid ounces (¹/₄ cup) dry white
    wine
2 sun-dried tomato halves
    (not packed in oil), minced
¹/₄ cup minced fresh flat-leaf parsley
1 bay leaf

1. In a food processor, pulse the tomatoes and their juice several times to chop coarsely; set aside.

2. Place a large saucepan over medium-high heat 30 seconds; heat the oil 30 seconds more. Add the onion; cook, stirring frequently, about 2 minutes, until softened. Add the celery and carrot; cook 2 minutes more, until the vegetables are slightly wilted.

3. Add the beef and cook, stirring constantly to break up the meat, about 5 minutes, until no longer pink; season with salt and pepper. Add the wine, reduce the heat to medium and cook about 4 minutes, until most of the liquid is evaporated. Add the reserved tomatoes, sun-dried tomatoes, parsley and bay leaf; cook, stirring until the sauce begins to bubble. Immediately reduce the heat to low and simmer, uncovered, stirring occasionally, 30 minutes, until thickened. Remove and discard the bay leaf before serving.

Serving (¹/₂ cup) provides: ¹/₂ Fat, 1¹/₂ Vegetables, ³/₄ Protein, 15 Optional Calories.

Per Serving: 115 Calories, 5 g Total Fat, 1 g Saturated Fat, 18 mg Cholesterol, 182 mg Sodium, 8 g Total Carbohydrate, 2 g Dietary Fiber, 7 g Protein, 45 mg Calcium.

Tomato Sauce

Simplicity itself, this sauce is at the heart of many a memorable pasta dish. Double, triple or even quadruple this recipe and freeze it in $^{1}/_{2}$-cup portions so you'll always have some on hand.

Makes 4 servings

1 tablespoon + 1 teaspoon olive oil
3 cups chopped seeded peeled plum
  tomatoes, with their juice*
1 garlic clove, minced

$^{1}/_{4}$ teaspoon salt
Freshly ground black pepper, to
  taste

Place a medium nonstick saucepan over medium heat 30 seconds; heat the oil 30 seconds more. Add the tomatoes, garlic, salt and pepper; cook, stirring frequently, 13–15 minutes, until thickened.

Serving (about $^{1}/_{2}$ cup) provides: 1 Fat, $1^{1}/_{2}$ Vegetables.

Per Serving: 69 Calories, 5 g Total Fat, 1 g Saturated Fat, 0 mg Cholesterol, 147 mg Sodium, 7 g Total Carbohydrate, 2 g Dietary Fiber, 1 g Protein, 9 mg Calcium.

If fresh plum tomatoes are not available, substitute an equal amount of chopped drained canned Italian plum tomatoes (no salt added).

TOMATO-HERB SAUCE

This sauce enlivens even the plainest pasta, meat, fowl, fish or vegetable fare. It's fast and easy to make on the spur of the moment, and it also freezes well.

Makes 4 servings

- 1 tablespoon + 1 teaspoon olive oil
- 3 cups chopped seeded peeled plum tomatoes, with their juice*
- 2 tablespoons minced fresh flat-leaf parsley
- 2 tablespoons minced fresh basil (or 1 teaspoon dried)
- 1 tablespoon minced fresh oregano (or 1 teaspoon dried)
- 2 teaspoons minced fresh thyme leaves (or $^1/_2$ teaspoon dried)
- 1 garlic clove, minced
- $^1/_4$ teaspoon salt
- Freshly ground black pepper, to taste

Place a medium nonstick saucepan over medium heat 30 seconds; heat the oil 30 seconds more. Add the tomatoes, parsley, basil, oregano, thyme, garlic, salt and pepper; cook, stirring frequently, 13–15 minutes, until thickened.

Serving ($^1/_2$ cup) provides: 1 Fat, 1$^1/_2$ Vegetables.

Per Serving: 72 Calories, 5 g Total Fat, 1 g Saturated Fat, 0 mg Cholesterol, 148 mg Sodium, 7 g Total Carbohydrate, 2 g Dietary Fiber, 1 g Protein, 29 mg Calcium.

*If fresh plum tomatoes are not available, substitute an equal number of chopped drained canned plum tomatoes (no salt added).

ANTIPASTI

Roasted Pepper and Mozzarella Bocconcini

Fennel with Balsamic Vinegar and Shaved Parmesan Cheese

Clams Oreganato

Clams Casino

Caponata

Sun-Dried Tomato and Mozzarella Crostini

Chèvre, Tomato and Basil Crostini

Crab Crostini

Fresh Tomato Crostini

Sun-Dried Tomato Crostini

Bruschetta

ROASTED PEPPER AND MOZZARELLA BOCCONCINI

Smoky-sweet peppers, creamy cheese and pungent herbs make this an irresistible appetizer.

Makes 4 servings

1 medium green bell pepper, roasted* (juices reserved) and cut into 1" strips
1 medium red bell pepper, roasted* (juices reserved) and cut into 1" strips
1 medium yellow bell pepper, roasted* (juices reserved) and cut into 1" strips
$^1/_2$ fluid ounce (1 tablespoon) dry white wine

2 teaspoons olive oil
1 teaspoon dried oregano
1 teaspoon dried basil
1 teaspoon dried thyme leaves
1 teaspoon white wine vinegar
1 garlic clove, minced
Freshly ground black pepper, to taste
6 ounces skim-milk mozzarella cheese, cut into 24 equal cubes

1. In a large bowl, combine the reserved pepper juices with the wine, oil, oregano, basil, thyme, vinegar, garlic and black pepper; add the mozzarella and toss to coat. Cover and let stand 30 minutes.
2. Drain the mozzarella cubes; discard liquid. Wrap each with a pepper strip and secure with a toothpick. Arrange on serving platter.

Serving (6 cubes) provides: $^1/_2$ Fat, $1^1/_2$ Vegetables, 2 Proteins, 5 Optional Calories.

Per Serving: 106 Calories, 2 g Total Fat, 0 g Saturated Fat, 4 mg Cholesterol, 317 mg Sodium, 7 g Total Carbohydrate, 1 g Dietary Fiber, 14 g Protein, 329 mg Calcium.

To roast bell peppers, preheat the broiler. Line a baking sheet or pie pan with foil; set whole peppers onto the prepared baking sheet. Broil the peppers 4–6" from heat, turning frequently with tongs, until skin is lightly charred on all sides. Transfer peppers to a clean paper bag; fold top down and let peppers steam 10 minutes. Peel, seed and devein peppers over a bowl to catch juices.

FENNEL WITH BALSAMIC VINEGAR AND SHAVED PARMESAN CHEESE

Raw or cooked, fennel is a popular vegetable in Italy. Its sweet, subtle, licorice-like flavor goes perfectly with balsamic vinegar and Parmesan cheese.

Makes 4 servings

2 medium fennel bulbs, trimmed and sliced into rings
4 teaspoons extra virgin olive oil
2 teaspoons balsamic vinegar

$^3/_4$ ounce Parmesan cheese
Freshly ground black pepper, to taste

1. Rinse the fennel in cold water; drain and pat dry with paper towels. Divide evenly among 4 salad plates. Drizzle each portion with 1 teaspoon of the oil and $^1/_2$ teaspoon of the balsamic vinegar.
2. With a vegetable peeler, cheese knife or the slicing side of a box grater, shave very thin slices of the cheese. Place an equal amount of the cheese on each portion of fennel; sprinkle with the pepper. Serve at room temperature or slightly chilled.

Serving (1 cup) provides: 1 Fat, 2 Vegetables, $^1/_4$ Protein.

Per Serving: 82 Calories, 6 g Total Fat, 2 g Saturated Fat, 4 mg Cholesterol, 201 mg Sodium, 3 g Total Carbohydrate, 1 g Dietary Fiber, 3 g Protein, 123 mg Calcium.

CLAMS OREGANATO

This recipe, which minimizes the bread crumbs and maximizes the briny flavor of the clams, will make some of the best baked clams you've ever had.

Makes 4 servings

12 medium clams, scrubbed
2 fluid ounces (¹/₄ cup) dry white wine
2 large or 4 small plum tomatoes, peeled, seeded and chopped
¹/₂ cup chopped white mushrooms
3 tablespoons plain dried bread crumbs
2 tablespoons minced fresh flat-leaf parsley
2 tablespoons fresh lemon juice
1 tablespoon + 1 teaspoon olive oil

1 tablespoon minced fresh oregano (or ¹/₂ teaspoon dried)
1 tablespoon minced fresh thyme leaves (or ¹/₂ teaspoon dried leaves, crumbled)
2 garlic cloves, minced
Freshly ground black pepper, to taste
2 teaspoons freshly grated Parmesan cheese
4 lemon wedges, to garnish

1. Line a 13 × 9" baking pan with foil, shiny side up. Preheat the broiler.
2. In a large saucepan over medium heat, combine the clams and wine. Cover and cook 4–5 minutes, until the clams open. Discard any unopened clams. When cool enough to handle, remove the clams from their shells. Reserve 12 shells; reserve the cooking liquid separately.
3. In a food processor, combine the clams, 2–4 tablespoons of the cooking liquid, the tomatoes, mushrooms, bread crumbs, parsley, juice, oil, oregano, thyme, garlic and pepper. Pulse 4–5 times, just enough to chop the clams coarsely and blend the ingredients. Transfer to a medium bowl; if the mixture seems too dry, stir in 1 tablespoon cooking liquid at a time, until the mixture reaches the desired consistency.
4. Divide the mixture evenly among the 12 shells, pressing into place with a fork; sprinkle evenly with the cheese. Place the shells into the prepared baking pan and broil about 5 minutes, until the filling is browned and crisp. Divide evenly among 4 plates and serve, garnished with lemon wedges.

Serving (3 clams) provides: 1 Fat, ³/₄ Vegetable, ¹/₂ Protein, ¹/₄ Bread, 20 Optional Calories.

Per Serving: 109 Calories, 5 g Total Fat, 1 g Saturated Fat, 10 mg Cholesterol, 83 mg Sodium, 8 g Total Carbohydrate, 1 g Dietary Fiber, 5 g Protein, 54 mg Calcium.

CLAMS CASINO

If you can find them, use Cherrystone or littleneck clams—they have the best flavor.

Makes 4 servings

12 medium clams, scrubbed
2 fluid ounces ($^1/_4$ cup) dry white wine
2 teaspoons olive oil
$^1/_2$ cup minced Italian frying pepper
$^1/_2$ medium onion, minced
1 garlic clove, minced
$^1/_2$ large or 1 small plum tomato, peeled, seeded and chopped
3 tablespoons plain dried bread crumbs

2 tablespoons minced fresh flat-leaf parsley
1 tablespoon minced fresh oregano (or $^1/_2$ teaspoon dried)
1 tablespoon minced fresh basil (or $^1/_2$ teaspoon dried)
Freshly ground black pepper, to taste
3 slices bacon, crisp-cooked and crumbled
4 lemon wedges, to garnish

1. Line a 13 × 9" baking pan with foil, shiny side up. Preheat the broiler.
2. In a large saucepan over medium heat, combine the clams and wine. Cover and cook 4–5 minutes, until the clams open. Discard any unopened clams. When cool enough to handle, remove the clams from their shells and coarsely chop. Reserve 12 shells; reserve the cooking liquid separately.
3. Place a medium nonstick skillet over medium heat 30 seconds; heat the oil 30 seconds more. Add the frying pepper, onion and garlic; cook, stirring frequently, about 5 minutes, until the onion is golden.
4. In a food processor, combine the clams, $^1/_4$–$^1/_3$ cup of the cooking liquid, the tomatoes, bread crumbs, parsley, oregano, basil and black pepper. Pulse 4–5 times, just enough to chop the clams coarsely and blend the ingredients. Transfer to a medium bowl. Stir in the bacon and the frying pepper mixture.
5. Divide the mixture evenly among the 12 shells. Place the shells into the prepared baking pan and broil about 5 minutes, until the filling is browned and crisp. Divide evenly among 4 plates and serve, garnished with lemon wedges.

Serving (3 clams) provides: $^1/_2$ Fat, $^1/_2$ Vegetable, $^1/_2$ Protein, $^1/_4$ Bread, 40 Optional Calories.

Per Serving: 114 Calories, 5 g Total Fat, 1 g Saturated Fat, 14 mg Cholesterol, 139 mg Sodium, 8 g Total Carbohydrate, 1 g Dietary Fiber, 6 g Protein, 43 mg Calcium.

CAPONATA

Eggplant, celery, onions, and tomatoes are sauteed, then marinated in a sweet and sour sauce that gives this Sicilian dish the flavor and consistency of relish or chutney. It makes a great appetizer, spread or accompaniment to grilled meats—invent your own uses for it!

Makes 4 servings

1 tablespoon + 1 teaspoon olive oil
8 medium celery stalks, chopped
2 medium onions, chopped
1 garlic clove, minced
1 large eggplant, trimmed and coarsely chopped (do not peel)
4 large or 8 small plum tomatoes, peeled, seeded and chopped
1 cup low-sodium tomato juice

20 imported small black olives, pitted and chopped
2 tablespoons rinsed drained capers
3 tablespoons red wine vinegar
Sugar substitute to equal 2 tablespoons sugar
$^1/_4$ teaspoon salt
Freshly ground black pepper, to taste

1. Place a large nonstick skillet over medium heat 30 seconds; heat the oil 30 seconds more. Add the celery, onions and garlic and cook, stirring frequently, about 3 minutes, until the onion is softened.
2. Add the eggplant, tomatoes, juice, 1 cup of hot water, the olives and capers; cover and cook, stirring frequently and adding $^1/_2$ cup water at a time as needed, 20–30 minutes, until the vegetables are tender and the sauce is thickened. Stir in the vinegar, sugar substitute, salt and pepper; reduce the heat to low and cook, stirring frequently, 5 minutes. Serve at room temperature, or store in the refrigerator for up to 5 days.

Serving ($^3/_4$ cup) provides: $1^1/_2$ Fats, 5 Vegetables.

Per Serving: 153 Calories, 7 g Total Fat, 1 g Saturated Fat, 0 mg Cholesterol, 440 mg Sodium, 23 g Total Carbohydrate, 5 g Dietary Fiber, 4 g Protein, 117 mg Calcium.

SUN-DRIED TOMATO AND MOZZARELLA CROSTINI

Italians like to save their appetites for their meals, but when they want a *spuntino*, a little something to nibble with their wine, crostini are the answer. These little canapé-like treats may remind you of cocktail pizzas.

Makes 4 servings

8 sun-dried tomato halves,
    not packed in oil
1/2 large or 1 small plum tomato,
    chopped
1 tablespoon low-sodium tomato
    juice
2 teaspoons olive oil
1 garlic clove, minced

4 ounces crusty Italian bread,
    cut into eight 1/2-ounce slices
    and toasted
1 1/2 ounces skim-milk mozzarella
    cheese, shredded
1/4 teaspoon dried thyme leaves,
    crumbled
1/4 teaspoon dried oregano

1. Line the broiler pan with foil, shiny side up. Preheat the broiler.
2. In a food processor or blender, purée the sun-dried tomatoes, plum tomato, juice, oil and garlic until smooth.
3. Place the bread slices on the prepared broiler pan. Spread 1 teaspoon of the tomato mixture on each slice of bread.
4. Sprinkle the mozzarella, thyme and oregano evenly over the tomato mixture. Broil 1 minute, until the cheese is melted and bubbling. Serve at once.

Serving (2 slices) provides: 1/2 Fat, 1 Vegetable, 1/2 Protein, 1 Bread.

Per Serving: 130 Calories, 3 g Total Fat, 1 g Saturated Fat, 1 mg Cholesterol, 250 mg Sodium, 18 g Total Carbohydrate, 2 g Dietary Fiber, 7 g Protein, 102 mg Calcium.

CHÈVRE, TOMATO AND BASIL CROSTINI

Chèvre is more French than Italian, but its delicious flavor and lower fat content take it across culinary borders. Garden fresh tomatoes and basil make these crostini irresistible.

Makes 4 servings

1¹/₂ ounces chèvre (goat cheese)

4 ounces crusty Italian bread, cut into eight ¹/₂-ounce slices and toasted

4 small plum tomatoes, each cut into 4 slices

¹/₄ teaspoon salt

Freshly ground black pepper, to taste

8 fresh basil leaves

Spread the chèvre evenly over the bread slices; lay 2 slices of the tomato, slightly overlapping if necessary, over each. Sprinkle evenly with salt and pepper and top each with a basil leaf. Serve at room temperature.

Serving (2 slices) provides: ¹/₂ Vegetable, ¹/₂ Protein, 1 Bread.

Per Serving: 121 Calories, 4 g Total Fat, 2 g Saturated Fat, 8 mg Cholesterol, 358 mg Sodium, 16 g Total Carbohydrate, 1 g Dietary Fiber, 5 g Protein, 60 mg Calcium.

CRAB CROSTINI

If crabmeat is out of your price range, surimi makes an excellent substitute.

Makes 4 servings

4 ounces fresh or frozen cooked
  crabmeat
2 tablespoons finely diced celery
1 tablespoon slivered basil leaves
1 tablespoon fresh lemon juice

2 teaspoons extra virgin olive oil
$^1/_4$ teaspoon salt
$^1/_8$ teaspoon ground red pepper
4 ounces Italian bread, cut into
  eight $^1/_2$-ounce slices

1. In a medium bowl, combine the crabmeat, celery, basil, juice, oil, salt and pepper. Cover and refrigerate 2 hours; remove from the refrigerator 1 hour before serving.
2. Preheat the oven to 400° F. Place the bread slices on a baking sheet and bake 10–12 minutes, until lightly browned. Divide the crab mixture evenly among the bread slices and serve.

Serving (2 slices) provides: $^1/_2$ Fat, $^1/_2$ Protein, 1 Bread.

Per Serving: 128 Calories, 4 g Total Fat, 1 g Saturated Fat, 28 mg Cholesterol, 383 mg Sodium, 15 g Total Carbohydrate, 1 g Dietary Fiber, 8 g Protein, 60 mg Calcium.

FRESH TOMATO CROSTINI

Crusty bread, tomatoes, garlic, and parsley evoke picnics in the Italian country-side. Create your own *pranzino al fresco* (little outdoor lunch) with these crostini, some fresh fruit and wine or mineral water.

Makes 4 servings

2 medium tomatoes, chopped
1/4 cup minced fresh parsley
2 teaspoons extra virgin olive
    oil
1 garlic clove, minced

Freshly ground black pepper,
    to taste
4 ounces crusty Italian peasant
    bread, cut into four 1-ounce
    slices and toasted

1. In a medium bowl, combine the tomatoes, parsley, oil, garlic and pepper. Cover and let stand 30 minutes.
2. Divide the tomato mixture, with its juices, evenly among the bread slices. Serve at room temperature.

Serving (1 slice) provides: 1/2 Fat, 1 Vegetable, 1 Bread.

Per Serving: 115 Calories, 4 g Total Fat, 1 g Saturated Fat, 0 mg Cholesterol, 174 mg Sodium, 18 g Total Carbohydrate, 2 g Dietary Fiber, 3 g Protein, 32 mg Calcium.

SUN-DRIED TOMATO CROSTINI

Try this version of crostini when fresh tomatoes aren't in season—or if you can't get enough of sun-dried tomatoes, make it year 'round.

Makes 4 servings

16 sun-dried tomato halves
   (not packed in oil)
$^1/_2$ cup boiling water
$^1/_2$ cup fresh flat-leaf parsley
2 garlic cloves

2 teaspoons olive oil
$^1/_4$ teaspoon salt
4 ounces crusty Italian peasant
   bread, cut into eight $^1/_2$-ounce
   slices

1. In a small bowl, combine the tomatoes and water; soak 10–15 minutes, until softened. Drain the tomatoes; reserve the liquid separately.
2. In a food processor or blender, combine the tomatoes, parsley, 1 garlic clove and 1 tablespoon of the reserved tomato liquid. Process until smooth, using a spatula to scrape mixture from sides of bowl. Stir in the oil and salt; set aside.
3. Heat a cast-iron stovetop grill over high heat or preheat the broiler. With a metal spatula, press the bread onto the pan and grill 1 minute on each side; or broil the bread, 5" from heat, 1 minute on each side. Cut the remaining garlic in half; rub one side of each bread slice with cut side of garlic. Divide the tomato mixture evenly among the bread slices and serve.

Serving (2 slices) provides: $^1/_2$ Fat, 2 Vegetables, 1 Bread.

Per Serving: 131 Calories, 3 g Total Fat, 1 g Saturated Fat, 0 mg Cholesterol, 314 mg Sodium, 21 g Total Carbohydrate, 3 g Dietary Fiber, 5 g Protein, 35 mg Calcium.

BRUSCHETTA

In Italian, this is called "anointed bread." Fruity extra virgin olive oil lends its unmistakable flavor to this most basic—and delectable—of appetizers.

Makes 4 servings

4 ounces crusty Italian peasant bread, cut into four 1-ounce slices and toasted
1 large garlic clove, halved
2 teaspoons extra virgin olive oil
2 teaspoons freshly grated Parmesan cheese

2 teaspoons minced fresh flat-leaf parsley
Freshly ground black pepper, to taste

1. While it is still warm, rub each slice of toast with a cut side of the garlic clove.
2. Drizzle evenly with the oil; then sprinkle evenly with the cheese, parsley and pepper.

Serving (1 slice) provides: $^1/_2$ Fat, 1 Bread, 5 Optional Calories.

Per Serving: 103 Calories, 4 g Total Fat, 1 g Saturated Fat, 1 mg Cholesterol, 185 mg Sodium, 15 g Total Carbohydrate, 1 g Dietary Fiber, 3 g Protein, 39 mg Calcium.

3

SOUPS

Lentil Soup

In addition to its great taste, this versatile soup freezes well, makes a fantastic pasta sauce, especially on curly pasta, and is low in fat, high in fiber. It makes a perfect vegetarian meal.

Makes 8 servings

2 teaspoons olive oil
2 medium onions, diced
1 garlic clove, minced
15 ounces lentils, rinsed and
   drained
2 medium carrots, diced
4 medium celery stalks, diced
2 cups sliced well-washed trimmed
   leeks
1¹/₂ cups canned Italian plum
   tomatoes (no salt added),
   drained, finely chopped and
   ¹/₂ cup juice reserved

2 tablespoons red wine vinegar
1 tablespoon minced fresh sage
   leaves
1 bay leaf
¹/₄ teaspoon salt
Freshly ground black pepper,
   to taste

1. Place a large nonstick saucepan or Dutch oven over medium heat 30 seconds; heat the oil 30 seconds more. Add the onions and garlic and cook, stirring frequently, 5 minutes, until the onions are golden. Add the lentils and 8 cups of water. Bring the liquid to a boil; add the carrots, celery and leeks. Cover and reduce the heat to low; simmer, stirring occasionally, about 45 minutes, until the lentils and vegetables are tender.
2. Stir in the tomatoes and the ¹/₂ cup juice, the vinegar, sage, bay leaf, salt and pepper; add another 1–2 cups of water, a little at a time as needed. Cover and simmer 30 minutes more, stirring frequently. Remove and discard the bay leaf. Divide evenly among 8 bowls and serve.

Serving (1¹/₄ cups) provides: ¹/₄ Fat, 2¹/₄ Vegetables, 2¹/₂ Proteins.

Per Serving: 253 Calories, 2 g Total Fat, 0 g Saturated Fat, 0 mg Cholesterol, 109 mg Sodium, 44 g Total Carbohydrate, 9 g Dietary Fiber, 17 g Protein, 80 mg Calcium.

RIBOLLITA

Twice-Cooked Soup

Ribollita means "reboiled," and as with any soup worthy of such a name, it is much better the next day. Authentic Ribollita includes black cabbage, which is virtually unavailable on American shores, but kale makes a fine substitute.

Makes 8 servings

12 ounces dry cannellini (white kidney) beans, picked over, rinsed and drained

8 cups chopped well-washed trimmed kale

2 teaspoons olive oil

2 medium onions, chopped

1 ounce well-trimmed Canadian-style bacon, julienned

2 garlic cloves, minced

3 cups canned Italian plum tomatoes (no salt added), drained, chopped and 1 cup juice reserved

4 medium celery stalks, chopped

1 medium carrot, chopped

2 tablespoons minced fresh sage leaves (or 2 teaspoons dried)

$1/4$ teaspoon salt

Freshly ground black pepper, to taste

2 tablespoons extra virgin olive oil

1. In a large bowl, combine the beans and cold water to cover; soak overnight.
2. Drain and rinse the beans and transfer to a large saucepan; add cold water to cover. Bring to a simmer over medium heat; cover and cook about 1 hour, until barely tender. Drain and rinse the beans. In a food processor, purée half the beans; return the pureed beans to the saucepan; cover and set aside.
3. In a large pot, bring 2" water to a boil. Arrange the kale on a steamer rack; place in the pot and cover with a tight-fitting lid. Steam 3–5 minutes, until tender.
4. Place a large nonstick saucepan or Dutch oven over medium heat 30 seconds; heat the oil 30 seconds more. Add the onions, bacon and garlic and cook, stirring frequently, about 2 minutes, until the onions are softened. Stir in the tomatoes and the 1 cup juice, celery and carrot; reduce the heat to low and simmer 5 minutes more, until the celery and carrot are softened.

5. Add the beans, 8 cups of water, the kale, sage, salt and pepper to the tomato mixture. Bring the liquid to a boil; reduce the heat to low and simmer, stirring frequently, about 30 minutes, until the beans and kale are very tender and the soup is thickened. Cool to room temperature; cover and refrigerate several hours or overnight.

6. Thirty minutes before serving, reheat the soup over low heat to a gentle boil. Divide evenly among 8 bowls; drizzle $^3/_4$ teaspoon oil over each portion and serve.

Serving (2 cups) provides: 1 Fat, $3^3/_4$ Vegetables, 2 Proteins, 10 Optional Calories.

Per Serving: 263 Calories, 6 g Total Fat, 1 g Saturated Fat, 2 mg Cholesterol, 191 mg Sodium, 41 g Total Carbohydrate, 11 g Dietary Fiber, 15 g Protein, 202 mg Calcium.

MINESTRONE

Bursting with vegetables, beans and pasta, minestrone is a meal in itself. Make it for a crowd, or freeze half for another time.

Makes 8 servings

6 ounces dry cannellini (white kidney) beans, picked over, rinsed and drained
8 cups low-sodium beef broth
$1/4$ teaspoon salt
Freshly ground black pepper, to taste
2 teaspoons olive oil
2 medium onions, chopped
1 medium carrot, diced
2 medium celery stalks, chopped
1 garlic clove, minced

3 cups canned Italian plum tomatoes (no salt added), drained, chopped and 1 cup juice reserved
$1/2$ cup minced fresh parsley
3 cups coarsely chopped green cabbage
2 medium zucchini, diced
3 ounces ditalini or other small pasta
1 tablespoon + 1 teaspoon freshly grated Parmesan cheese

1. In a large bowl, combine the beans with cold water to cover; soak overnight.
2. Drain and rinse the beans and transfer to a large saucepan; add the broth, salt and pepper. Bring to a simmer over medium heat; cover and cook about 1 hour, until barely tender.
3. Meanwhile, place a large nonstick skillet over medium heat 30 seconds; heat the oil 30 seconds more. Add the onions, carrot, celery and garlic; cook, stirring frequently, about 3 minutes, until the onion is softened.
4. Stir the vegetable mixture into the bean mixture; add the tomatoes, the 1 cup juice and parsley. Reduce the heat to medium-low and simmer 20 minutes. Add the cabbage, zucchini and pasta and cook 12–15 minutes more, until the cabbage is tender. Remove from heat; cover and let stand 10 minutes. Divide evenly among 8 bowls; sprinkle each portion with $1/2$ teaspoon cheese and serve.

Serving (1 cup) provides: $1/4$ Fat, $2^3/4$ Vegetables, 1 Protein, $1/2$ Bread, 25 Optional Calories.

Per Serving: 197 Calories, 2 g Total Fat, 0 g Saturated Fat, 1 mg Cholesterol, 197 mg Sodium, 32 g Total Carbohydrate, 5 g Dietary Fiber, 14 g Protein, 113 mg Calcium.

PASTA E FAGIOLI

PASTA AND BEAN SOUP

Make this hearty pasta and bean soup a day ahead; the soup will thicken and the flavors will blend. It will be well worth the wait.

Makes 4 servings

1 tablespoon + 1 teaspoon olive oil

$^1/_2$ medium carrot, chopped

1 medium onion, chopped

2 medium celery stalks, chopped

1 ounce well-trimmed Canadian-style bacon, diced

20 ounces rinsed drained canned cannellini (white kidney) beans

3 cups low-sodium beef broth

2 cups canned Italian plum tomatoes (no salt added), drained, chopped and 1 cup juice reserved

6 ounces tubetti pasta or elbow macaroni

$^1/_4$ teaspoon salt

Freshly ground black pepper, to taste

$^3/_4$ ounce Parmesan cheese, grated

2 tablespoons minced fresh sage leaves (or 1 teaspoon dried)

1. Place a large nonstick saucepan or Dutch oven over medium heat 30 seconds; heat the oil 30 seconds more. Add the onion and cook about 5 minutes, until golden. Add the celery, carrot and bacon and cook, stirring frequently, about 5 minutes more, until the celery and carrot are softened. Add the beans, broth, tomatoes and juice; bring to a boil. Reduce the heat to medium-low and simmer, stirring frequently, 15 minutes, until slightly thickened.
2. In a food processor or blender, purée 1 cup of beans with a little of the cooking liquid; return to the saucepan. Bring to a low boil.
3. Stir in tubetti, salt and pepper; cook, stirring, 5–6 minutes, until the pasta is tender but still firm. Cool; cover and refrigerate overnight.
4. Thirty minutes before serving, reheat the soup over low heat, adding $^1/_2$ cup water at a time, until the soup reaches the desired consistency. Divide evenly among 4 bowls; sprinkle each portion evenly with cheese and sage and serve.

Serving (1$^1/_2$ cups) provides: 1 Fat, 1$^3/_4$ Vegetables, 3 Proteins, 2 Breads, 15 Optional Calories.

Per Serving: 467 Calories, 9 g Total Fat, 2 g Saturated Fat, 8 mg Cholesterol, 724 mg Sodium, 70 g Total Carbohydrate, 13 g Dietary Fiber, 27 g Protein, 198 mg Calcium.

ESCAROLE SOUP

Chicken broth, escarole and cheese combine to make this soup light yet hearty. Even though it doesn't take much time to prepare, it tastes like something that's been simmering all day.

Makes 4 servings

1 medium head escarole, cored, trimmed, washed and chopped
6 cups low-sodium chicken broth

4 teaspoons freshly grated Parmesan cheese
Freshly ground black pepper, to taste

1. In a large saucepan or skillet over low heat, combine the escarole and $1/4$ cup water; cover and cook, checking frequently to make sure that some liquid remains and adding a little water if necessary, about 5 minutes, until the escarole is wilted and tender. Drain and squeeze out excess moisture; set aside.
2. In the same saucepan, over medium-high heat, bring the broth to a boil; add the escarole. Reduce the heat to medium-low and simmer, stirring occasionally, 10 minutes, until the escarole is very tender. Divide evenly among 4 bowls; sprinkle each portion with 1 teaspoon cheese and the pepper and serve.

Serving ($1^{1}/_{2}$ cups) provides: 3 Vegetables, 40 Optional Calories.

Per Serving: 58 Calories, 4 g Total Fat, 2 g Saturated Fat, 2 mg Cholesterol, 226 mg Sodium, 5 g Total Carbohydrate, 2 g Dietary Fiber, 7 g Protein, 89 mg Calcium.

MINESTRA DI ZUCCA

SQUASH SOUP

When most people think of squash in Italian cooking, they think of zucchini. But in Mantua, near Venice and Verona, the yellow winter squash *zucca gialla* is a staple. One favorite preparation is this thick, rich soup, where pureed squash is delicately flavored with sage and, instead of prosciutto, Canadian-style bacon.

Makes 4 servings

One 2¹/₂-pound butternut squash, pared, seeded and coarsely chopped
1 tablespoon + 1 teaspoon olive oil
1 medium onion, chopped
1 ounce well-trimmed Canadian-style bacon, diced

3 cups low-sodium chicken broth
Freshly ground black pepper, to taste
4 teaspoons minced fresh sage leaves (or 1¹/₄ teaspoons dried)

1. In a large saucepan, bring 2" water to a boil. Arrange the squash on a steamer rack; place in the saucepan and cover with a tight-fitting lid. Steam 15 minutes, until tender; set aside.
2. Place a large nonstick saucepan over medium heat 30 seconds; heat the oil 30 seconds more. Add the onion and bacon and cook, stirring frequently, about 5 minutes, until the onion is light golden. Add the squash and broth and bring to a boil. Reduce the heat to low; cover and simmer 10–15 minutes, until the squash is very tender.
3. In a food processor, purée the squash mixture until smooth. Return the purée to the saucepan and add the pepper. Cook, stirring frequently, 1–2 minutes, to make sure the soup is heated through. Divide evenly among 4 bowls; sprinkle each with 1 teaspoon sage and serve.

Serving (1 cup) provides: 1 Fat, ¹/₄ Vegetable, ¹/₄ Protein, ¹/₂ Bread, 25 Optional Calories.

Per Serving: 185 Calories, 7 g Total Fat, 1 g Saturated Fat, 4 mg Cholesterol, 196 mg Sodium, 31 g Total Carbohydrate, 5 g Dietary Fiber, 7 g Protein, 135 mg Calcium.

Spinach and Rice Soup

Arborio rice takes a holiday from risotto in this somewhat thick chicken soup, giving it extra heft and nutrition.

Makes 4 servings

1 pound 4 ounces well-washed trimmed spinach

1 tablespoon + 1 teaspoon reduced-calorie tub margarine

1/2 medium onion, chopped

4 cups low-sodium chicken broth

3 1/2 ounces Arborio rice

4 teaspoons freshly grated Parmesan cheese

1. In a large saucepan, cook the spinach with just the water that clings to the leaves from washing, covered, 2–3 minutes, until the leaves are wilted and the liquid is boiling. Drain over a bowl; reserve liquid.

2. Place a large nonstick saucepan over medium heat 30 seconds; melt the margarine 30 seconds more. Add the onion and cook, stirring frequently, about 3 minutes, until softened. Add the spinach and cook, stirring constantly, 2 minutes more, until wilted.

3. Add the broth and reserved spinach liquid and bring to a boil. Stir in the rice and cook, stirring occasionally, about 30 minutes, until tender. Divide evenly among 4 bowls; sprinkle each portion with 1 teaspoon cheese and serve.

Serving (1 1/4 cups) provides: 1/2 Fat, 2 Vegetables, 1 Bread, 35 Optional Calories.

Per Serving: 179 Calories, 6 g Total Fat, 2 g Saturated Fat, 1 mg Cholesterol, 287 mg Sodium, 27 g Total Carbohydrate, 4 g Dietary Fiber, 10 g Protein, 183 mg Calcium.

Tortellini in Brodo

Little Dumplings in Broth

In some parts of Italy, these are called *cappelletti* (little caps); in other parts they are called *tortellini* (little cakes). Making them can be a family project; so can eating them. Vary this recipe by using your favorite fillings and broths.

Makes 4 servings

8 cups low-sodium vegetable broth
48 Meat-Filled Tortellini
(page 4)

4 teaspoons freshly grated Parmesan cheese

1. In a large saucepan over medium-high heat, bring the broth to a boil; add the tortellini. When the broth returns to a boil, reduce the heat to low and simmer about 10 minutes, until the tortellini are tender but still firm around the edges.
2. Divide evenly among 4 bowls; sprinkle each portion with 1 teaspoon cheese and serve.

Serving (12 tortellini with 2 cups broth) provides: $3/4$ Fat, $1 3/4$ Proteins, $2 1/4$ Breads, 55 Optional Calories.

Per Serving: 427 Calories, 12 g Total Fat, 4 g Saturated Fat, 182 mg Cholesterol, 591 mg Sodium, 56 g Total Carbohydrate, 1 g Dietary Fiber, 22 g Protein, 174 mg Calcium.

4

PASTAS

Pasta with Vegetables: *Spaghetti with Fresh Basil and Tomatoes • Penne with Broccoli*
Perciatelli alla Boscaiola • Tagliatelle with Artichoke Hearts and Tomatoes
Farfalle with Lemon and Herbs • Fusilli with Pureed Yellow Pepper Sauce
Rotelle with Greens • Fettuccine with Walnut Sauce • Penne Arrabiata
Spaghettini con Aglio e Olio • Linguine with Herbed "Butter"
Orecchiette with Broccoli Rabe and Cannellini • Fettuccine Alfredo
Farfalle with Asparagus • Ziti with Cabbage, Onions and Balsamic Vinegar
Penne with Vodka Cream Sauce

Pasta with Fish and Seafood: *Capellini with Seafood • Pasta Shells with Clams*
and Broccoli • Spaghetti alla Puttanesca
Farfalle with Grilled Swordfish and Vegetables • Linguine with Red Clam Sauce
Linguine with White Clam Sauce • Spaghettini with Mussels Marinara
Spaghettini with Mussels, Garlic and White Wine • Linguine with Sun-Dried Tomatoes,
Chèvre and Basil
Fusilli with Spinach, Ricotta Cheese and Raisins • Rigatoni with Three Cheeses
Lasagna with Tomatoes, Ricotta, Mozzarella and Parmesan

Pasta with Meat and Poultry: *Spaghetti Carbonara • Ziti with Tomatoes, Peppers,*
Onions and Sausage
Perciatelli all'Amatriciana • Rigatoni with Sausage and Fennel
Spaghetti with Meatballs • Pappardelle with Meat Sauce

SPAGHETTI WITH FRESH BASIL AND TOMATOES

Throughout Italy, nothing says summer as much as fresh-picked tomatoes and basil still warm from the sun. This sauce is not cooked; the heat from the pasta brings forth the flavors of the vegetables, so use the freshest vine-ripened tomatoes you can find.

Makes 4 servings

4 large or 8 small plum tomatoes, peeled, seeded and chopped	$^1/_4$ teaspoon salt
1 tablespoon + 1 teaspoon extra virgin olive oil	Freshly ground black pepper, to taste
1 garlic clove, bruised	6 ounces spaghetti
	$^1/_2$ cup minced fresh basil

1. In a large serving bowl, combine the tomatoes, oil, garlic, salt and pepper.
2. In a large pot of boiling water, cook the spaghetti according to package directions. Drain; set aside and keep warm.
3. Remove and discard the garlic from the tomato mixture; Add the spaghetti and toss gently to coat; sprinkle with the basil. Divide evenly among 4 plates and serve.

Serving (1$^1/_2$ cups) provides: 1 Fat, 1 Vegetable, 2 Breads.

Per Serving: 215 Calories, 6 g Total Fat, 1 g Saturated Fat, 0 mg Cholesterol, 144 mg Sodium, 36 g Total Carbohydrate, 2 g Dietary Fiber, 6 g Protein, 60 mg Calcium.

PENNE WITH BROCCOLI

Pasta and broccoli are a popular duo in Italy. In this recipe, anchovies and pine nuts play supporting roles.

Makes 4 servings

4 cups bite-size broccoli florets
6 ounces penne
1 cup low-sodium chicken or
  vegetable broth
1 tablespoon + 1 teaspoon olive oil
1 medium onion, chopped
2 garlic cloves, minced

1 tablespoon + 1 teaspoon pine nuts
2 rinsed drained anchovy fillets
  (or 1 teaspoon anchovy paste)
$1/4$ teaspoon crushed red pepper
  flakes
1 tablespoon + 1 teaspoon freshly
  grated Parmesan cheese

1. In a large saucepan, bring 2" water to a boil. Arrange the broccoli on a steamer rack; place in the saucepan and cover with a tight-fitting lid. Steam 5 minutes, until tender-crisp. Set aside and keep warm.
2. In a large pot of boiling water, cook the penne according to package directions. Drain and place in a serving bowl; keep warm.
3. Meanwhile, in a large nonstick skillet, bring $1/2$ cup of the broth and the oil to a simmer over medium heat. Add the onion and garlic; cook, stirring frequently, 2 minutes, until the onion is softened. Add the pine nuts, anchovies and pepper flakes; cook, stirring constantly, 1 minute, until thoroughly blended. Stir in the broccoli and remaining $1/2$ cup of broth; cook, stirring frequently, 5 minutes, until the liquid is reduced by half. Add to the bowl with the penne and toss to coat; sprinkle with the cheese. Divide evenly among 4 plates and serve at once.

Serving (2 cups) provides: $1^1/4$ Fats, $2^1/4$ Vegetables, 2 Breads, 25 Optional Calories.

Per Serving: 283 Calories, 8 g Total Fat, 2 g Saturated Fat, 3 mg Cholesterol, 175 mg Sodium, 42 g Total Carbohydrate, 6 g Dietary Fiber, 13 g Protein, 108 mg Calcium.

PERCIATELLI ALLA BOSCAIOLA

PERCIATELLI WOODSMAN'S STYLE

Wild mushrooms give this dish the woodsy flavor of an autumn dish. Perciatelli (also called *bucatini*) is a long hollow pasta; if you can't find it, substitute spaghetti.

Makes 4 servings

1 ounce dried porcini mushrooms
1 tablespoon + 1 teaspoon olive oil
2 ounces well-trimmed prosciutto
   or lean boiled ham, chopped
2 garlic cloves, minced
4 large or 8 small plum tomatoes,
   peeled, seeded and chopped*
2 cups white mushrooms, cut into
   $1/4$" slices

2 cups shiitake mushrooms,
   cut into $1/4$" slices
$1/4$ cup minced fresh flat-leaf parsley
$1/4$ teaspoon salt
Freshly ground black pepper,
   to taste
6 ounces perciatelli pasta

1. In a small bowl, combine the porcini with warm water to cover; soak 30 minutes, until softened. Strain the mushrooms through a cheesecloth-lined strainer; reserve the mushrooms and the liquid separately.
2. Place a large nonstick skillet over medium heat 30 seconds; heat the oil 30 seconds more. Add the prosciutto and garlic and cook 1 minute, stirring constantly. Add the porcini and soaking liquid; increase the heat to medium-high and cook, stirring frequently, 3–5 minutes, until all the liquid is evaporated.
3. Add the tomatoes, white and shiitake mushrooms, parsley, salt and pepper. Reduce the heat to medium and cook, stirring occasionally, 15 minutes, until thickened. Set aside and keep warm.
4. Meanwhile, in a large pot of boiling water, cook the perciatelli according to package directions. Drain and place in a serving bowl. Add the sauce and toss to blend. Divide evenly among 4 plates and serve.

Serving ($1^3/4$ cups) provides: 1 Fat, $2^1/4$ Vegetables, $1/2$ Protein, 2 Breads.

Per Serving: 275 Calories, 8 g Total Fat, 1 g Saturated Fat, 12 mg Cholesterol, 411 mg Sodium, 42 g Total Carbohydrate, 4 g Dietary Fiber, 12 g Protein, 26 mg Calcium.

If fresh plum tomatoes are not available, substitute an equal number of chopped drained canned Italian plum tomatoes (no salt added).

TAGLIATELLE WITH ARTICHOKE HEARTS AND TOMATOES

Elegant enough for company, hearty enough for a family meal and simple to prepare, this is sure to become part of your regular repertoire.

Makes 4 servings

2 cups frozen artichoke hearts
(10-ounce package)
6 ounces tagliatelle pasta
1 tablespoon + 1 teaspoon olive oil
1 medium onion, finely chopped
1 garlic clove, minced
4 large or 8 small plum tomatoes,
peeled, seeded and chopped*

¹/₄ teaspoon salt
Freshly ground black pepper,
to taste
¹/₄ cup minced fresh flat-leaf parsley
1 tablespoon + 1 teaspoon freshly
grated Parmesan cheese

1. Cook the artichoke hearts according to package directions, until tender. Cut into bite-size pieces. Transfer to a serving bowl; set aside and keep warm.
2. In a large pot of boiling water, cook the tagliatelle according to package directions. Drain and place in the serving bowl with the artichoke hearts and keep warm.
3. Meanwhile, place a medium nonstick skillet over medium heat 30 seconds; heat the oil 30 seconds more. Add the onion and garlic; cook 2 minutes, until the onion is softened. Add the tomatoes; cook, stirring occasionally, 10 minutes, until mixture is thickened. Add to the bowl with the tagliatelle and artichokes; toss to coat. Sprinkle with the parsley and cheese. Divide evenly among 4 plates and serve.

Serving (2 cups) provides: 1 Fat, 2¹/₄ Vegetables, 2 Breads, 10 Optional Calories.

Per Serving: 255 Calories, 6 g Total Fat, 1 g Saturated Fat, 2 mg Cholesterol, 216 mg Sodium, 42 g Total Carbohydrate, 5 g Dietary Fiber, 9 g Protein, 63 mg Calcium.

*If fresh plum tomatoes are not available, substitute an equal number of chopped drained canned Italian plum tomatoes (no salt added).

FARFALLE WITH LEMON AND HERBS

Here's something light for a summer luncheon.

Makes 4 servings

¹/₄ cup minced fresh flat-leaf parsley
¹/₄ cup minced fresh basil
¹/₄ cup minced fresh mint leaves
Zest of 1 lemon, finely grated*
2 tablespoons fresh lemon juice
2 teaspoons reduced-calorie tub
    margarine, melted
2 teaspoons olive oil

¹/₄ teaspoon salt
¹/₄ teaspoon ground white pepper
6 ounces farfalle (bow tie) pasta
¹/₄ cup low-sodium chicken broth,
    hot
1 tablespoon + 1 teaspoon freshly
    grated Parmesan cheese
Fresh herb sprigs, to garnish

1. In a medium serving bowl, combine the parsley, basil, mint, zest, juice, margarine, oil, salt and pepper; set aside.
2. In a large pot of boiling water, cook the farfalle according to package directions. Drain and add to the bowl with the herb mixture. Add the broth and cheese; toss lightly to coat. Garnish with fresh herb sprigs. Divide evenly among 4 plates and serve.

Serving (1 cup) provides: ³/₄ Fat, 2 Breads, 10 Optional Calories.

Per Serving: 208 Calories, 5 g Total Fat, 1 g Saturated Fat, 2 mg Cholesterol, 199 mg Sodium, 34 g Total Carbohydrate, 1 g Dietary Fiber, 7 g Protein, 70 mg Calcium.

The zest of the lemon is the peel without any of the pith (white membrane). To remove zest from lemon, use a zester or the fine side of a vegetable grater.

FUSILLI WITH PUREED YELLOW PEPPER SAUCE

To turn this lovely sauce into a flavorful dip for a crudité platter, substitute 4 ounces nonfat cream cheese for the ricotta.

Makes 4 servings

1 large yellow bell pepper, seeded
  and chopped
1 medium onion, chopped
$^{1}/_{2}$ medium tomato, chopped
2 teaspoons olive oil
$^{1}/_{4}$ teaspoon salt
Freshly ground black pepper,
  to taste

6 ounces fusilli pasta
$^{1}/_{4}$ cup part-skim ricotta cheese
2 tablespoons minced fresh parsley
1 tablespoon + 1 teaspoon freshly
  grated Parmesan cheese

1. In a large nonstick skillet over medium-low heat, combine $^{3}/_{4}$ cup water, the bell pepper, onion, tomato, oil, salt and black pepper. Cover and cook, stirring frequently and adding $^{1}/_{4}$ cup water at a time as needed, 15–18 minutes, until the vegetables are tender and the liquid is evaporated.
2. Meanwhile, in a large pot of boiling water, cook the fusilli according to package directions. Drain and place in a serving bowl; keep warm.
3. In a blender or food processor, combine the pepper mixture and ricotta cheese; purée until smooth. Add to the bowl with the fusilli and toss to coat. Sprinkle with the parsley and Parmesan cheese. Divide evenly among 4 plates and serve.

Serving (1$^{1}/_{2}$ cups) provides: $^{1}/_{2}$ Fat, 1$^{1}/_{2}$ Vegetables, $^{1}/_{4}$ Protein, 2 Breads, 10 Optional Calories.

Per Serving: 233 Calories, 5 g Total Fat, 2 g Saturated Fat, 6 mg Cholesterol, 199 mg Sodium, 38 g Total Carbohydrate, 2 g Dietary Fiber, 9 g Protein, 90 mg Calcium.

ROTELLE WITH GREENS

Here's an easy and delicious way to get your vegetables—garlic and lemon give the whole dish real pizazz.

Makes 4 servings

1 tablespoon + 1 teaspoon olive oil
2 medium onions, chopped
1 garlic clove, chopped
$^1/_2$ cup low-sodium chicken broth
8 cups coarsely chopped well-washed trimmed spinach
2 cups coarsely chopped well-washed trimmed Swiss chard
$^1/_4$ teaspoon salt
Freshly ground black pepper, to taste
6 ounces rotelle (wheel) pasta
$^1/_2$ tablespoon fresh lemon juice

1. Place a large nonstick skillet over medium-high heat 30 seconds; heat the oil 30 seconds more. Add the onions and garlic; cook, stirring frequently, about 5 minutes, until the onions are golden. Add the broth; cook 3–4 minutes, until most of the broth is evaporated.
2. Meanwhile, in a large saucepan, bring 2" water to a boil. Arrange the spinach and Swiss chard on a steamer rack; place in the saucepan and cover with a tight-fitting lid. Steam 5–6 minutes, until the greens are tender.
3. Remove the greens from the steamer; squeeze out any excess moisture. Stir into the onion mixture and season with salt and pepper. Cook, stirring frequently, 1 minute. Set aside and keep warm.
4. Meanwhile, in a large pot of boiling water, cook the rotelle according to package directions. Drain and place in a large serving bowl. Add the greens mixture, sprinkle with the juice and toss to combine. Divide evenly among 4 plates and serve.

Serving (1$^1/_2$ cups) provides: 1 Fat, 5$^1/_2$ Vegetables, 2 Breads, 5 Optional Calories.

Per serving: 246 Calories, 6 g Total Fat, 1 g Saturated Fat, 0 mg Cholesterol, 281 mg Sodium, 41 g Total Carbohydrate, 5 g Dietary Fiber, 10 g Protein, 141 mg Calcium.

FETTUCCINE WITH WALNUT SAUCE

A creamy walnut sauce with flecks of parsley makes this a festive dish. Round out the meal with Sauteed Peppers (page 135) or Arugula and Radicchio Salad with Balsamic Vinegar and Crumbled Parmesan Cheese (page 104).

Makes 4 servings

$^1/_2$ cup part-skim ricotta cheese
$^1/_4$ cup low-sodium chicken broth
1 teaspoon grated lemon zest*
6 ounces fettuccine
1 ounce chopped walnuts

$^3/_4$ ounce Gorgonzola cheese, crumbled
2 tablespoons minced fresh flat-leaf parsley

1. In a small bowl, combine the ricotta cheese, broth and zest; mix until smooth. Set aside.
2. In a large pot of boiling water, cook the fettuccine according to package directions. Drain and place in a serving bowl. Top with the ricotta mixture; sprinkle with walnuts, Gorgonzola cheese and parsley. Toss to coat. Divide evenly among 4 plates and serve.

Serving (1 cup) provides: $^1/_2$ Fat, 1 Protein, 2 Breads.

Per Serving: 271 Calories, 10 g Total Fat, 3 g Saturated Fat, 55 mg Cholesterol, 129 mg Sodium, 33 g Total Carbohydrate, 2 g Dietary Fiber, 12 g Protein, 136 mg Calcium.

The zest of the lemon is the peel without any of the pith (white membrane). To remove zest from lemon, use a zester or the fine side of a vegetable grater.

PENNE ARRABIATA

ENRAGED QUILLS

This Roman dish gets its name from the hot pepper that flavors it. Adjust the amount of pepper flakes to suit your comfort level.

Makes 4 servings

1 tablespoon + 1 teaspoon olive oil
1 medium onion, finely chopped
6 large or 12 small plum tomatoes, peeled, seeded and chopped*
2 garlic cloves, minced

$^1/_2$ teaspoon crushed red pepper flakes
$^1/_4$ teaspoon salt
6 ounces penne
Fresh parsley sprigs, to garnish

1. Place a medium nonstick skillet over medium heat 30 seconds; heat the oil 30 seconds more. Add the onion and cook, stirring frequently, 2 minutes, until softened. Add the tomatoes, garlic, pepper flakes and salt. Cook, stirring occasionally, 10 minutes, until the mixture is thickened. Set aside and keep warm.
2. Meanwhile, in a large pot of boiling water, cook the penne according to package directions. Drain and place in a serving bowl; add the sauce and toss to coat. Divide evenly among 4 plates and serve, garnished with parsley.

Serving ($1^1/_2$ cups) provides: 1 Fat, $1^3/_4$ Vegetables, 2 Breads.

Per Serving: 225 Calories, 5 g Total Fat, 1 g Saturated Fat, 0 mg Cholesterol, 146 mg Sodium, 38 g Total Carbohydrate, 2 g Dietary Fiber, 6 g Protein, 20 mg Calcium.   4 pts

*If fresh plum tomatoes are not available, substitute an equal number of chopped drained canned Italian plum tomatoes (no salt added).

Spaghettini con Aglio e Olio

Spaghettini with Garlic and Oil

Popular as an evening snack with Roman revelers, this humble, easy and savory dish wins points for being a great standby when the cupboard is bare. A side dish of crunchy vegetables makes it a satisfying meal.

Makes 4 servings

6 ounces spaghettini
$1/3$ cup + 2 teaspoons low-sodium chicken broth
1 tablespoon + 1 teaspoon olive oil
2 garlic cloves, minced

$1/8$ teaspoon crushed red pepper flakes
2 tablespoons minced fresh flat-leaf parsley

1. In a large pot of boiling water, cook the spaghettini according to package directions. Drain and place in a serving bowl; keep warm.
2. In a medium nonstick skillet over medium heat, combine the broth, oil, garlic and pepper flakes. Cook, stirring constantly, 1–2 minutes, until the mixture is heated through and the garlic starts to sizzle and becomes fragrant. Pour over the spaghettini and sprinkle with the parsley; toss to coat. Divide evenly among 4 plates and serve.

Serving (1 cup) provides: 1 Fat, 2 Breads.

Per Serving: 203 Calories, 5 g Total Fat, 1 g Saturated Fat, 0 mg Cholesterol, 15 mg Sodium, 33 g Total Carbohydrate, 1 g Dietary Fiber, 6 g Protein, 14 mg Calcium.

LINGUINE WITH HERBED "BUTTER"

Reduced-calorie margarine is the perfect "carrier" for herbs—especially since it has half the calories and fat of butter.

Makes 4 servings

2 tablespoons + 2 teaspoons
   reduced-calorie tub margarine
2 tablespoons minced fresh parsley
1 tablespoon minced fresh basil
1 tablespoon minced fresh thyme
   leaves
1 tablespoon minced fresh oregano
1 garlic clove, bruised
$1/4$ teaspoon salt
Freshly ground black pepper,
   to taste
6 ounces linguine

1. In a large pot of boiling water, cook the linguine according to package directions. Drain and place in a serving bowl; keep warm.
2. Place a small nonstick skillet over medium heat 30 seconds; melt the margarine 30 seconds more. Add the parsley, basil, thyme, oregano, garlic, salt and pepper. Reduce the heat to low and cook 30 seconds, until the herbs wilt. Remove and discard the garlic. Pour the herb mixture over the linguine and toss to coat. Divide evenly among 4 plates and serve at once.

Serving (1 cup) provides: 1 Fat, 2 Breads.

Per Serving: 208 Calories, 6 g Total Fat, 1 g Saturated Fat, 0 mg Cholesterol, 196 mg Sodium, 33 g Total Carbohydrate, 1 g Dietary Fiber, 6 g Protein, 28 mg Calcium.

ORECCHIETTE WITH BROCCOLI RABE AND CANNELLINI

Broccoli rabe and cannellini are traditional with orecchiette, but the combination of bitter green and creamy bean tastes wonderful with any pasta.

Makes 4 servings

6 cups coarsely chopped well-washed trimmed broccoli rabe
1 tablespoon + 1 teaspoon olive oil
1 medium onion, coarsely chopped
$^1/_2$ cup low-sodium vegetable broth
4 garlic cloves, minced
$^1/_4$ teaspoon salt

$^1/_4$ teaspoon crushed red pepper flakes
16 ounces rinsed drained canned cannellini (white kidney) beans
1 teaspoon fresh lemon juice
6 ounces orecchiette pasta
1 tablespoon + 1 teaspoon freshly grated Parmesan cheese

1. In a large saucepan, bring 2" water to a boil. Arrange the broccoli rabe on a steamer rack; place in the saucepan and cover with a tight-fitting lid. Steam 10 minutes, until tender.
2. Place a large nonstick skillet over medium heat 30 seconds; heat the oil 30 seconds more. Add the onion; cook, stirring frequently, 5 minutes, until golden. Add the broccoli rabe, broth, garlic, salt and pepper flakes; cook, stirring occasionally, 5 minutes, until most of the liquid is evaporated. Add the beans and juice; cook, stirring frequently, 1 minute. Set aside and keep warm.
3. Meanwhile, in a large pot of boiling water, cook the orecchiette according to package directions. Drain and place in a serving bowl. Add the broccoli rabe mixture; sprinkle with the cheese and toss to combine. Divide evenly among 4 plates and serve.

Serving (2 cups) provides: 1 Fat, $3^1/_4$ Vegetables, 2 Proteins, 2 Breads, 15 Optional Calories.

Per Serving: 368 Calories, 7 g Total Fat, 1 g Saturated Fat, 2 mg Cholesterol, 443 mg Sodium, 59 g Total Carbohydrate, 10 g Dietary Fiber, 18 g Protein, 119 mg Calcium.

FETTUCCINE ALFREDO

Parmesan cheese, mushrooms, and just a bit of cream make this lightened sauce as rich-tasting as the original. Because this lightened rendition is still fairly high in fat, save this dish for an occasional splurge.

Makes 4 servings

6 ounces fettuccine
1 tablespoon + 1 teaspoon
   reduced-calorie tub margarine
Freshly ground black pepper,
   to taste

$^1/_4$ cup heavy cream
$^3/_4$ ounce Parmesan cheese, grated
1 large white mushroom, cut into
   paper-thin slices

1. Spray a large nonstick skillet with nonstick cooking spray.
2. In a large pot of boiling water, cook the fettuccine according to package directions. Drain and place in the skillet.
3. Place the skillet over medium heat. Add the margarine and pepper and toss gently. Add the cream and toss gently, until it is heated through and most of it is absorbed.
4. Add the cheese and mushroom slices and toss gently 2–3 minutes, until the pasta is evenly coated with melted cheese. Divide evenly among 4 plates and serve at once.

Serving (1 cup) provides: $^1/_2$ Fat, $^1/_4$ Protein, 2 Breads, 50 Optional Calories.

Per Serving: 265 Calories, 12 g Total Fat, 5 g Saturated Fat, 65 mg Cholesterol, 142 mg Sodium, 31 g Total Carbohydrate, 1 g Dietary Fiber, 9 g Protein, 97 mg Calcium.

FARFALLE WITH ASPARAGUS

This pasta dish truly celebrates spring! Farfalle and asparagus are tossed with a light, creamy sauce that's the next best thing to the first robin's song. Add a salad or entrée that features other seasonal specialties and you'll be well on your way to a healthful case of spring fever.

Makes 4 servings

24 medium asparagus spears, trimmed and cut diagonally into 1" pieces
6 ounces farfalle (bow tie) pasta
2 tablespoons + 2 teaspoons reduced-calorie tub margarine
3 medium shallots, chopped
1/4 cup low-sodium chicken broth
1/4 cup light cream
1/4 teaspoon salt
Freshly ground black pepper, to taste
1 tablespoon + 1 teaspoon freshly grated Parmesan cheese

1. In a large saucepan, bring 2" water to a boil. Arrange the asparagus on a steamer rack; place in the saucepan and cover with a tight-fitting lid. Steam 6 minutes, until tender; set aside and keep warm.
2. In a large pot of boiling water, cook the farfalle according to package directions. Drain and place in a large serving bowl; keep warm.
3. Meanwhile, place a medium nonstick skillet over medium heat 30 seconds; melt the margarine 30 seconds more. Add the shallots; cook, stirring frequently, 2 minutes, until softened. Reduce the heat to low; add the broth and cream and cook, stirring constantly, about 10 minutes, until reduced by half; do *not* let the mixture boil. Add to the bowl with the farfalle, sprinkle with salt and pepper and toss to coat. Top evenly with the asparagus and cheese. Divide evenly among 4 plates and serve at once.

Serving (1¹/₂ cups) provides: 1 Fat, 1 Vegetable, 2 Breads, 40 Optional Calories.

Per Serving: 271 Calories, 10 g Total Fat, 3 g Saturated Fat, 12 mg Cholesterol, 249 mg Sodium, 37 g Total Carbohydrate, 2 g Dietary Fiber, 10 g Protein, 74 mg Calcium.

ZITI WITH CABBAGE, ONIONS AND BALSAMIC VINEGAR

The Venetians use cabbage in many dishes. This sweet and sour pasta dish is a nice complement to pork.

Makes 4 servings

1 tablespoon + 1 teaspoon olive oil	2 teaspoons fennel seeds
2 medium red onions, chopped	$^1/_4$ teaspoon salt
8 cups shredded green cabbage	Freshly ground black pepper,
1 cup low-sodium chicken broth	to taste
2 garlic cloves, minced	6 ounces ziti
1 tablespoon balsamic vinegar	

1. Place a large nonstick saucepan over medium heat 30 seconds; heat the oil 30 seconds more. Add the onions; cook, stirring frequently, 5 minutes, until golden. Add the cabbage, broth and garlic; cook, stirring occasionally, 5 minutes, until the cabbage is wilted. Add the vinegar, fennel seeds, salt and pepper. Reduce the heat to low; cover and simmer 20 minutes, until the cabbage is tender. Remove the cover, increase the heat to medium and cook 5 minutes more, until the liquid is evaporated.
2. Meanwhile, in a large pot of boiling water, cook the ziti according to package directions. Drain and place in a serving bowl. Add the cabbage mixture and toss to combine. Divide evenly among 4 plates and serve.

Serving (1 cup) provides: 1 Fat, $4^1/_2$ Vegetables, 2 Breads, 5 Optional Calories.

Per Serving: 260 Calories, 6 g Total Fat, 1 g Saturated Fat, 0 mg Cholesterol, 198 mg Sodium, 45 g Total Carbohydrate, 5 g Dietary Fiber, 9 g Protein, 105 mg Calcium.

PENNE WITH VODKA CREAM SAUCE

Sauced with cream, tomato and vodka, this lightened version of a real restaurant favorite is thought by many Americans to be an invention of nouvelle cuisine. The Italians claim, however, that they've been enjoying it for years. Stewed Artichokes (page 146) or Sauteed Broccoli with Garlic and Lemon (page 132) makes a nice accompaniment.

Makes 4 servings

6 ounces penne
2 tablespoons + 2 teaspoons
   reduced-calorie tub margarine
3 medium shallots, finely chopped
¹/₄ cup low-sodium chicken broth
1 tablespoon tomato paste
   (no salt added)
¹/₄ teaspoon crushed red pepper
   flakes

¹/₄ cup heavy cream
1 fluid ounce (2 tablespoons) vodka
2 tablespoons minced fresh flat-leaf
   parsley
1 tablespoon + 1 teaspoon freshly
   grated Parmesan cheese

1. In a large pot of boiling water, cook the penne according to package directions. Drain and place in a serving bowl; keep warm.
2. Place a medium nonstick skillet over medium heat 30 seconds; melt the margarine 30 seconds more. Add the shallots; cook, stirring frequently, 2–3 minutes, until softened. Add the broth, tomato paste and pepper flakes; cook, stirring constantly, about 1 minute, until combined.
3. Reduce the heat to low. Add the cream and vodka; cook, stirring constantly, 2 minutes, until heated through; do *not* let the mixture boil. Pour the sauce over the penne and toss to coat. Sprinkle with the parsley and cheese. Divide evenly among 4 plates and serve.

Serving (1 cup) provides: 1 Fat, ¹/₄ Vegetable, 2 Breads, 80 Optional Calories.

Per Serving: 295 Calories, 12 g Total Fat, 5 g Saturated Fat, 22 mg Cholesterol, 115 mg Sodium, 35 g Total Carbohydrate, 1 g Dietary Fiber, 7 g Protein, 54 mg Calcium.

CAPELLINI WITH SEAFOOD

Shrimp, scallops, mussels and clams in a light briny broth nestle among delicate strands of pasta flecked with herbs. Treat yourself well and use the freshest seafood you can find.

Makes 4 servings

12 medium clams, scrubbed

12 medium mussels, scrubbed and debearded

2 fluid ounces (¹/₄ cup) dry white wine

2 garlic cloves, minced

2 teaspoons olive oil

8 ounces bay scallops, rinsed and drained

5 ounces medium shrimp (about 12), peeled and deveined

2 tablespoons minced fresh parsley

1 tablespoon minced fresh thyme leaves

1 tablespoon minced fresh oregano

6 ounces capellini (angel hair) pasta

Freshly ground black pepper, to taste

1. In a large saucepan over medium heat, combine the clams, mussels, wine and garlic. Cover and cook 4–5 minutes, until the clams and mussels open. Discard any unopened clams and mussels. Set aside with the cooking liquid.

2. Place a large nonstick skillet over medium heat 30 seconds; heat the oil 30 seconds more. Add the scallops, shrimp, parsley, thyme and oregano. Cook, stirring constantly, 2–3 minutes, until the shrimp are pink and the scallops are opaque. Remove from the heat and add the clam mixture to the scallop mixture; set aside and keep warm.

3. Meanwhile, in a large pot of boiling water, cook the capellini according to package directions. Drain and place in a serving bowl. Add the seafood mixture and sprinkle with pepper; toss to combine. Divide evenly among 4 plates and serve at once.

Serving (1 cup) provides: ¹/₂ Fat, 2¹/₄ Proteins, 2 Breads, 15 Optional Calories.

Per Serving: 318 Calories, 5 g Total Fat, 1 g Saturated Fat, 80 mg Cholesterol, 236 mg Sodium, 36 g Total Carbohydrate, 1 g Dietary Fiber, 28 g Protein, 73 mg Calcium.

PASTA SHELLS WITH CLAMS AND BROCCOLI

Who would guess that two such unlikely ingredients could form such a magnificent partnership? Onion, garlic and just a hint of lemon maks it work. If you can't find tiny pasta shells, any small pasta will do.

Makes 4 servings

6 ounces tiny pasta shells
4 cups bite-size broccoli florets
24 medium clams, scrubbed
2 medium onions, chopped
4 fluid ounces ($^1/_2$ cup) dry white wine

1 tablespoon + 1 teaspoon olive oil
2 garlic cloves, minced
$^1/_2$ teaspoon crushed red pepper flakes
1 tablespoon fresh lemon juice

1. In a large pot of boiling water, cook the pasta shells according to package directions. Drain and place in a serving bowl; keep warm.

2. In a large saucepan, bring 2" water to a boil. Arrange the broccoli on a steamer rack; place in the saucepan and cover with a tight-fitting lid. Steam the broccoli florets 7 minutes, until tender but still bright green. Add to the pasta shells.

3. Meanwhile, in a large saucepan over medium heat, combine the clams, onions, wine, oil, garlic and pepper flakes. Cover and cook 4–5 minutes, until the clams open. Discard any unopened clams. When cool enough to handle, remove the clams from their shells and coarsely chop. Add them and the cooking liquid to the pasta shells and broccoli. Add the juice and toss to combine. Divide evenly among 4 plates and serve at once.

Serving (2 cups) provides: 1 Fat, $2^1/_2$ Vegetables, 1 Protein, 2 Breads, 25 Optional Calories.

Per Serving: 319 Calories, 6 g Total Fat, 1 g Saturated Fat, 19 mg Cholesterol, 69 mg Sodium, 45 g Total Carbohydrate, 6 g Dietary Fiber, 18 g Protein, 104 mg Calcium.

SPAGHETTI ALLA PUTTANESCA

Named for Italian "ladies of the night" who concocted it as a midnight snack, this tasty dish traditionally uses canned tuna. Prepared with fresh tuna, it's a truly superb entrée.

Makes 4 servings

6 ounces spaghetti
1 tablespoon olive oil
10 ounces tuna steak, cut into
   1" chunks
4 large or 8 small plum tomatoes,
   peeled, seeded and chopped*
6 pitted large ripe olives, chopped
1 tablespoon rinsed drained capers

2 garlic cloves, minced
2 rinsed drained anchovy fillets,
   minced (or 1 teaspoon anchovy
   paste)
¼ teaspoon crushed red pepper
   flakes
¼ cup minced fresh flat-leaf parsley

1. In a large pot of boiling water, cook the spaghetti according to package directions. Drain and place in a serving bowl; keep warm.
2. Meanwhile, place a large nonstick skillet over medium heat 30 seconds; heat the oil 30 seconds more. Add the tuna and cook, stirring frequently, about 5 minutes, until golden brown. Add the tomatoes, olives, capers, garlic, anchovies and pepper flakes; cook, stirring frequently, 10 minutes, until the mixture is thickened. Transfer to the bowl with the spaghetti and sprinkle with the parsley; toss to combine. Divide evenly among 4 plates and serve.

Serving (1¼ cups) provides: 1 Fat, 1 Vegetable, 1 Protein, 2 Breads, 5 Optional Calories.

Per Serving: 317 Calories, 9 g Total Fat, 2 g Saturated Fat, 28 mg Cholesterol, 227 mg Sodium, 35 g Total Carbohydrate, 2 g Dietary Fiber, 23 g Protein, 29 mg Calcium.

If fresh plum tomatoes are not available, substitute an equal number of chopped drained canned Italian plum tomatoes (no salt added).

FARFALLE WITH GRILLED SWORDFISH AND VEGETABLES

This is a perfect meal for a sultry summer evening. After marinating, the fish and vegetables are grilled; the farfalle can be cooked ahead of time and the whole dish served at room temperature.

Makes 4 servings

4 fluid ounces (¹/₂ cup) dry white wine
¹/₄ cup fresh lemon juice
¹/₄ cup low-sodium tomato juice
¹/₄ cup minced fresh parsley
1 tablespoon + 1 teaspoon olive oil
1 tablespoon minced fresh basil
1 tablespoon minced fresh oregano
1 tablespoon minced fresh thyme leaves
¹/₄ teaspoon salt

Freshly ground black pepper, to taste
10 ounces swordfish steak, cut into 1" cubes
1 medium green bell pepper, seeded and cut into 1" pieces
1 medium red bell pepper, seeded and cut into 1" pieces
8 small plum tomatoes, halved
6 ounces farfalle

1. In a small bowl, combine the wine, lemon juice, tomato juice, parsley, oil, basil, oregano, thyme, salt and black pepper.
2. To prepare the marinade, pour one-half of the wine mixture into a gallon-size sealable plastic bag, add the swordfish, green and red bell peppers and tomatoes. Cover and refrigerate the remaining wine mixture. Seal the bag, squeezing out air; turn to coat the fish and vegetables. Refrigerate at least 2 hours or overnight, turning the bag occasionally.
3. Soak three 12" bamboo skewers in water for 15 minutes. Spray the broiler or grill rack with nonstick cooking spray; place 5" from heat. Preheat the broiler, or prepare the grill according to the manufacturer's instructions.
4. Drain the fish and vegetables and discard the marinade. Thread the peppers, tomatoes and fish on separate skewers. Broil or grill the fish and vegetables about 10 minutes, turning once, until the pepper and tomato skins are charred and the fish is golden brown and cooked through. Remove from the skewers and transfer to a serving bowl. Add the remaining wine mixture and toss to coat.

5. Meanwhile, in a large pot of boiling water, cook the farfalle according to package directions. Drain and add to the vegetables and fish. Toss to combine. Divide evenly among 4 plates and serve hot or at room temperature.

Serving (1¹/₄ cups) provides: 1 Fat, 2 Vegetables, 1 Protein, 2 Breads, 25 Optional Calories.

Per Serving: 337 Calories, 8 g Total Fat, 1 g Saturated Fat, 28 mg Cholesterol, 212 mg Sodium, 40 g Total Carbohydrate, 3 g Dietary Fiber, 21 g Protein, 44 mg Calcium.

LINGUINE WITH RED CLAM SAUCE

Makes 4 servings

12 medium clams, scrubbed
2 fluid ounces ($^1/_4$ cup) dry white
   wine
1 tablespoon minced fresh thyme
   leaves
1 tablespoon minced fresh oregano
2 large garlic cloves, minced
$^1/_4$ teaspoon crushed red pepper
   flakes
1 tablespoon + 1 teaspoon olive oil

8 large or 16 small plum tomatoes,
   peeled, seeded and chopped*
$^1/_2$ cup chopped Italian frying
   pepper
$^1/_4$ cup finely minced fresh flat-leaf
   parsley
$^1/_4$ teaspoon salt
Freshly ground black pepper,
   to taste
6 ounces linguine

1. In a large saucepan over medium heat, combine the clams, wine, thyme, oregano, garlic and pepper flakes. Cover and cook 4–5 minutes, until the clams open. Discard any unopened clams. When cool enough to handle, remove the clams from their shells and coarsely chop; cover and set aside. Reserve the shells for garnish, if desired; reserve the cooking liquid separately.

2. Place a medium nonstick skillet over medium heat 30 seconds; heat the oil 30 seconds more. Add the tomatoes, frying pepper, parsley, salt and black pepper. Cook, stirring frequently, 5 minutes; add the reserved liquid. Reduce the heat to medium-low and simmer 5–10 minutes, until the sauce is thickened.

3. Meanwhile, in a large pot of boiling water, cook the linguine according to package directions. Drain and place in a serving bowl.

4. Stir the clams into the tomato mixture and cook 1 minute more, until heated through. Pour the sauce over the linguine and toss lightly to coat. Garnish with the clam shells, if desired. Divide evenly among 4 plates and serve.

Serving ($1^1/_2$ cups) provides: 1 Fat, $2^1/_4$ Vegetables, $^1/_2$ Protein, 2 Breads, 15 Optional Calories.

Per Serving: 264 Calories, 6 g Total Fat, 1 g Saturated Fat, 10 mg Cholesterol, 167 mg Sodium, 40 g Total Carbohydrate, 3 g Dietary Fiber, 11 g Protein, 49 mg Calcium.

*If fresh plum tomatoes are not available, substitute an equal number of chopped drained canned Italian plum tomatoes (no salt added).

Linguine with White Clam Sauce

If you lack the time or inclination to use fresh clams, substitute a 10-ounce can of whole baby clams, and skip Step 1.

Makes 4 servings

18 medium clams, scrubbed	4 garlic cloves, minced
4 fluid ounces ($^1/_2$ cup) dry white wine	$^1/_2$ cup minced fresh flat-leaf parsley
6 ounces linguine	$^1/_2$ teaspoon crushed red pepper flakes
1 tablespoon + 1 teaspoon olive oil	

1. In a large saucepan over medium heat, combine the clams and wine. Cover and cook 4–5 minutes, until the clams open. Discard any unopened clams. When cool enough to handle, remove the clams from their shells and coarsely chop; cover and set aside. Reserve shells for garnish, if desired; reserve the cooking liquid separately.

2. In a large pot of boiling water, cook the linguine according to package directions. Drain and place in a serving bowl; keep warm.

3. Meanwhile, place a large skillet over medium heat 30 seconds; heat the oil 30 seconds more. Add the garlic, parsley, pepper flakes and reserved liquid. Cook, stirring frequently, about 7 minutes, until the liquid is reduced by half. Add the clams to the skillet; cook, stirring frequently, 2 minutes, until heated through. Pour the sauce over the linguine and toss to coat. Garnish with the clam shells, if desired. Divide evenly among 4 plates and serve.

Serving (1$^1/_4$ cups) provides: 1 Fat, $^3/_4$ Protein, 2 Breads, 25 Optional Calories.

Per Serving: 257 Calories, 6 g Total Fat, 1 g Saturated Fat, 14 mg Cholesterol, 32 mg Sodium, 35 g Total Carbohydrate, 1 g Dietary Fiber, 11 g Protein, 45 mg Calcium.

SPAGHETTINI WITH MUSSELS MARINARA

Nothing evokes dining on the Mediterranean more clearly than this timeless dish. Tomatoes, garlic, olive oil and fresh, succulent mussels transport you to a seaside table, no matter where you live.

Makes 4 servings

6 ounces spaghettini

1 tablespoon + 1 teaspoon olive oil

1 cup canned Italian plum tomatoes (no salt added), drained and chopped

3 garlic cloves, minced

$^1/_2$ teaspoon crushed red pepper flakes

24 medium mussels, scrubbed and debearded

$^1/_3$ cup minced fresh flat-leaf parsley

1. In a large pot of boiling water, cook the spaghettini according to package directions. Drain and place in a serving bowl; keep warm.
2. Meanwhile, place a large saucepan over medium heat 30 seconds; heat the oil 30 seconds more. Add the tomatoes, garlic and pepper flakes; cook, stirring occasionally, about 2 minutes. Add the mussels; cover and cook 4–5 minutes, until the mussels open. Discard any unopened mussels. With a slotted spoon, transfer the mussels to a large bowl; set aside and keep warm.
3. Stir the parsley into the tomato mixture and cook about 5 minutes more, until the liquid is reduced by half. Return the mussels to the tomato sauce and cook about 2 minutes, until heated through. Pour the sauce over the spaghettini and toss to combine. Divide evenly among 4 plates and serve.

Serving (1 cup pasta with 6 mussels and $^1/_4$ cup sauce) provides: 1 Fat, $^1/_2$ Vegetable, 1 Protein, 2 Breads.

Per Serving: 252 Calories, 6 g Total Fat, 1 g Saturated Fat, 12 mg Cholesterol, 135 mg Sodium, 37 g Total Carbohydrate, 2 g Dietary Fiber, 11 g Protein, 45 mg Calcium.

SPAGHETTINI WITH MUSSELS, GARLIC AND WHITE WINE

Easy, quick, inexpensive, attractive, flavorful and filling—few dishes can boast so many attributes!

Makes 4 servings

6 ounces spaghettini
4 fluid ounces (¹/₂ cup) dry white wine
2 teaspoons olive oil
¹/₂ cup minced fresh flat-leaf parsley
1 tablespoon minced fresh thyme leaves (or 1 teaspoon dried leaves, crumbled)

4 garlic cloves, minced
¹/₄ teaspoon crushed red pepper flakes
24 medium-sized mussels, scrubbed and debearded

1. In a large pot of boiling water, cook the spaghettini according to package directions. Drain and place in a serving bowl; keep warm.
2. In a large saucepan over medium heat, combine the wine, oil, parsley, thyme, garlic and pepper flakes. Cook, stirring constantly, 1–2 minutes, until the garlic becomes fragrant. Add the mussels; cover and cook 4–5 minutes, until the mussels open. Discard any unopened mussels.
3. Add the mussel mixture to the spaghettini and toss to combine. Divide evenly among 4 plates and serve.

Serving (1¹/₂ cups) provides: ¹/₂ Fat, 1 Protein, 2 Breads, 25 Optional Calories.

Per Serving: 243 Calories, 4 g Total Fat, 1 g Saturated Fat, 12 mg Cholesterol, 130 mg Sodium, 35 g Total Carbohydrate, 1 g Dietary Fiber, 11 g Protein, 43 mg Calcium.

Linguine with Sun-Dried Tomatoes, Chèvre and Basil

A winning trio of flavors makes this no-cook sauce a summertime favorite.

Makes 4 servings

1¹/₂ cups packed fresh basil leaves
1 tablespoon + 1 teaspoon pine nuts
1 tablespoon olive oil
2 garlic cloves, minced
¹/₄ teaspoon salt
Freshly ground black pepper,
    to taste

16 sun-dried tomato halves
    (not packed in oil)
6 ounces linguine
2¹/₄ ounces herbed or plain chèvre
    (goat cheese), crumbled

1. In a food processor or blender, combine the basil, pine nuts, oil, garlic, salt and pepper. Purée until smooth; set aside.
2. In a small bowl, combine the tomatoes with warm water to cover; soak 10–15 minutes, until softened. Drain, discarding liquid; chop the tomatoes and set aside.
3. In a large pot of boiling water, cook the linguine according to package directions. Drain and place in a serving bowl. Add the basil mixture, tomatoes and chèvre and toss to coat. Divide evenly among 4 plates and serve.

Serving (1 cup) provides: 1 Fat, 2 Vegetables, ³/₄ Protein, 2 Breads, 10 Optional Calories.

Per Serving: 303 Calories, 10 g Total Fat, 4 g Saturated Fat, 13 mg Cholesterol, 232 mg Sodium, 42 g Total Carbohydrate, 3 g Dietary Fiber, 12 g Protein, 148 mg Calcium.

FUSILLI WITH SPINACH, RICOTTA CHEESE AND RAISINS

Spinach, ricotta and raisins are popular in southern Italy—it's one of those perfect combinations that gets even better when tossed with a curly pasta such as fusilli.

Makes 4 servings

2 tablespoons golden raisins
6 ounces fusilli pasta
2 cups thawed frozen chopped spinach (one 10-ounce package)
1 tablespoon + 1 teaspoon olive oil

1/2 medium onion, chopped
1/4 teaspoon salt
1 1/2 ounces Parmesan cheese, grated
1/4 cup part-skim ricotta cheese
1/4 teaspoon ground white pepper

1. In a small bowl, combine the raisins with warm water to cover; soak 10–15 minutes, until softened. Drain, discarding liquid, and set aside.
2. In a large pot of boiling water, cook the fusilli according to package directions. Drain and place in a serving bowl.
3. Meanwhile, cook the spinach according to package directions; drain, squeeze out excess liquid and set aside.
4. Place a medium nonstick skillet over medium heat 30 seconds; heat the oil 30 seconds more. Add the onion; cook 2 minutes, until softened. Reduce the heat to low; stir in the spinach and salt and cook 2 minutes, until wilted. Add the spinach mixture, raisins and Parmesan and ricotta cheeses to the fusilli; toss to combine and sprinkle with pepper. Divide evenly among 4 plates and serve.

Serving (1 1/4 cups) provides: 1 Fat, 1/4 Fruit, 1 Vegetable, 3/4 Protein, 2 Breads.

Per Serving: 302 Calories, 10 g Total Fat, 3 g Saturated Fat, 13 mg Total Cholesterol, 408 mg Sodium, 40 g Total Carbohydrate, 3 g Dietary Fiber, 14 g Protein, 280 mg Calcium.

Rigatoni with Three Cheeses

Mozzarella, Parmesan and fontina bring macaroni and cheese into a sophisticated—but still familiar—realm. To round out the meal and keep cleanup to a minimum, pop a vegetable casserole such as *Ciambotta* (page 144) in the oven, too.

Makes 4 servings

6 ounces rigatoni pasta
¹/₂ cup skim milk
1¹/₂ ounces skim-milk mozzarella
  cheese, shredded
1¹/₂ ounces fontina cheese, grated
¹/₄ cup minced fresh flat-leaf parsley

1 tablespoon minced fresh thyme
  leaves (or 1 teaspoon dried
  leaves, crumbled)
¹/₄ teaspoon ground white pepper
³/₄ ounce Parmesan cheese, grated

1. Preheat the oven to 425° F. Spray a 1-quart baking dish with nonstick cooking spray; set aside.
2. In a large pot of boiling water, cook the rigatoni according to package directions. Drain and return to the pot. Stir in the milk, mozzarella and fontina cheeses, parsley, thyme and pepper.
3. Spoon the rigatoni mixture into the prepared dish and sprinkle with the Parmesan. Bake 15–18 minutes, until golden and bubbling. Let stand 5 minutes. Divide evenly among 4 plates and serve.

Serving (1¹/₂ cups) provides: 1¹/₄ Proteins, 2 Breads, 10 Optional Calories.

Per Serving: 253 Calories, 6 g Total Fat, 3 g Saturated Fat, 18 mg Cholesterol, 283 mg Sodium, 35 g Total Carbohydrate, 1 g Dietary Fiber, 15 g Protein, 264 mg Calcium.

LASAGNA WITH TOMATOES, RICOTTA, MOZZARELLA AND PARMESAN

One of the most popular of Italian foods, lasagna is an indispensable part of any festive meal. Make a double recipe and freeze one for your next special occasion. Sauteed Broccoli with Garlic and Lemon (page 132) or a crunchy salad is a natural side dish.

Makes 8 servings

1 cup part-skim ricotta cheese
1¹/₂ ounces Parmesan cheese, grated
1 egg white
Freshly ground black pepper,
   to taste

9 ounces lasagna noodles
   (about 9 noodles)
2 cups Tomato Sauce (page [TK])
3 ounces skim-milk mozzarella
   cheese, shredded

1. In a small bowl, combine the ricotta and Parmesan cheeses, egg white and pepper; set aside.
2. Spray two 24" sheets of wax paper on one side with nonstick cooking spray.
3. In a large pot of boiling water, cook the lasagna noodles according to package directions. Drain and separate noodles; arrange in a single layer between the wax paper sheets.
4. Preheat the oven to 400° F. Spray a 13 × 9" baking dish with nonstick cooking spray.
5. Spread ¹/₂ cup of Tomato Sauce evenly over the bottom of the prepared dish, then add 3 lasagna noodles in a single layer, trimming the noodles as needed to fit the dish; reserve the trimmings for the next layer. Spread one third the ricotta mixture evenly over the noodles; drizzle with ¹/₂ cup of the Tomato Sauce and sprinkle with one third of the mozzarella and Parmesan cheeses. Add 3 more lasagna noodles and repeat the layers, ending with the Parmesan.
6. Cover with foil and bake 25 minutes; uncover and bake about 10 minutes more, until bubbling and slightly crispy on top. Let stand 5 minutes before cutting into 8 equal portions.

Serving (¹/₈ of the casserole) provides: ¹/₂ Fat, ³/₄ Vegetable, 1¹/₄ Proteins, 1¹/₂ Breads, 5 Optional Calories.

Per Serving: 237 Calories, 7 g Total Fat, 3 g Saturated Fat, 15 mg Cholesterol, 299 mg Sodium, 29 g Total Carbohydrate, 2 g Dietary Fiber, 14 g Protein, 242 mg Calcium.

SPAGHETTI CARBONARA

Egg substitute and Canadian-style bacon fill in for traditional eggs and pancetta (the delicate and very fatty Italian bacon)—but all the great taste is still here. Cannellini-Stuffed Peppers (page 138) or Sweet and Sour Onions (page 136) would be a great *contorno,* or side dish.

Makes 4 servings

2 ounces well-trimmed Canadian-style bacon, julienned
3 medium shallots, finely chopped
2 teaspoons olive oil
2 teaspoons reduced-calorie tub margarine
2 garlic cloves, bruised

6 ounces spaghetti
²/₃ cup fat-free egg substitute
1¹/₂ ounces Parmesan cheese, grated
1 tablespoon minced fresh flat-leaf parsley
Freshly ground black pepper, to taste

1. In a large nonstick skillet over medium heat, combine the bacon, shallots, oil, margarine and garlic. Cook 5 minutes, until the garlic is golden; remove and discard the garlic. Reserve the remaining ingredients in the skillet; set aside and keep warm.
2. Meanwhile, in a large pot of boiling water, cook the spaghetti according to package directions. Drain and add to the shallot mixture.
3. Return the bacon mixture to low heat. Add the egg substitute and cheese; toss to coat thoroughly. Transfer to a large serving bowl and sprinkle with the parsley and pepper. Divide evenly among 4 plates and serve.

Serving (³/₄ cup) provides: ³/₄ Fat, 1¹/₂ Proteins, 2 Breads.

Per Serving: 290 Calories, 8 g Total Fat, 3 g Saturated Fat, 15 mg Cholesterol, 484 mg Sodium, 35 g Total Carbohydrate, 1 g Dietary Fiber, 17 g Protein, 176 mg Calcium.

ZITI WITH TOMATOES, PEPPERS, ONIONS AND SAUSAGE

Here's a robust family-pleaser that's chock-full of flavor and texture. Italian turkey sausage is widely available in supermarkets; it's every bit as savory as—but much less fatty than—the pork-based version.

Makes 4 servings

1 tablespoon + 1 teaspoon olive oil
2 medium onions, coarsely chopped
4 Italian frying peppers, seeded, deveined and cut into 1" pieces
1 cup low-sodium tomato juice
4 ounces hot or sweet Italian turkey sausage, casing removed
2 garlic cloves, minced
$^1/_2$ cup chopped drained canned Italian plum tomatoes (no salt added)

1 tablespoon minced fresh oregano (or 1 teaspoon dried)
$^1/_4$ teaspoon salt
Freshly ground black pepper, to taste
6 ounces ziti
1 tablespoon + 1 teaspoon freshly grated Parmesan cheese

1. Place a large nonstick skillet over medium heat 30 seconds; heat the oil 30 seconds more. Add the onions; cook, stirring frequently, 2 minutes, until softened. Add the frying peppers and $^1/_2$ cup of the tomato juice; cook, stirring frequently, about 4 minutes, until the peppers start to soften. Add the sausage and garlic; cook, pressing with the back of a wooden spoon to break up the meat, 3–4 minutes, until the meat is no longer pink.
2. Add the tomatoes, the remaining $^1/_2$ cup tomato juice, the oregano, salt and black pepper. Reduce the heat to medium-low; cook, stirring frequently, about 8 minutes, until the vegetables are tender and the sauce is thickened.
3. Meanwhile, in a large pot of boiling water, cook the ziti according to package directions. Drain and place in a serving bowl. Add the sauce and cheese and toss to combine. Divide evenly among 4 plates and serve at once.

Serving (2 cups) provides: 1 Fat, $3^1/_4$ Vegetables, $^3/_4$ Protein, 2 Breads, 10 Optional Calories.

Per Serving: 323 Calories, 9 g Total Fat, 1 g Saturated Fat, 25 mg Cholesterol, 347 mg Sodium, 48 g Total Carbohydrate, 3 g Dietary Fiber, 14 g Protein, 82 mg Calcium.

Perciatelli all'Amatriciana

Perciatelli with Tomatoes and Bacon

With its smoky flavors and the zing of crushed red pepper, here's a perfect pasta for a blustery winter night. If you can't find perciatelli, which is a long hollow pasta that's sometimes called *bucatini*, substitute spaghetti.

Makes 4 servings

1 tablespoon + 1 teaspoon olive oil
1 medium onion, finely chopped
2 ounces well-trimmed Canadian-style bacon, diced
2 cups chopped drained canned Italian plum tomatoes (no salt added)

$^{1}/_{4}$ teaspoon crushed red pepper flakes
$^{1}/_{4}$ teaspoon salt
6 ounces perciatelli pasta
1 tablespoon + 1 teaspoon freshly grated Parmesan cheese

1. Place a large nonstick skillet over medium heat 30 seconds; heat the oil 30 seconds more. Add the onion and bacon; cook, stirring constantly, 5 minutes, until the onion is golden and the bacon is lightly browned. Add the tomatoes, pepper flakes and salt; cook, stirring frequently, about 15 minutes, until the sauce is thickened.
2. Meanwhile, in a large pot of boiling water, cook the perciatelli according to package directions. Drain and place in a serving bowl. Add the sauce and cheese and toss to combine. Divide evenly among 4 plates and serve.

Serving (1$^{1}/_{4}$ cups) provides: 1 Fat, 1$^{1}/_{4}$ Vegetables, $^{1}/_{2}$ Protein, 2 Breads, 10 Optional Calories.

Per Serving: 261 Calories, 7 g Total Fat, 1 g Saturated Fat, 9 mg Cholesterol, 392 mg Sodium, 39 g Total Carbohydrate, 2 g Dietary Fiber, 11 g Protein, 73 mg Calcium.

RIGATONI WITH SAUSAGE AND FENNEL

The spicy sausage and sweet fennel are balanced by the slightly tart tomato in this popular dish. We like it with rigatoni, but any sturdy pasta shape is suitable.

Makes 4 servings

1 tablespoon + 1 teaspoon olive oil
2 medium onions, chopped
1¹/₂ medium fennel bulbs, diced
1 garlic clove, minced
4 ounces hot or sweet Italian turkey sausage, casing removed
4 large or 8 small plum tomatoes, peeled, seeded and chopped*

¹/₂ teaspoon fennel seeds
¹/₄ teaspoon salt
Freshly ground black pepper, to taste
6 ounces rigatoni
2 teaspoons freshly grated Parmesan cheese

1. Place a large nonstick skillet over medium heat 30 seconds; heat the oil 30 seconds more. Add the onion, fennel and garlic; cook, stirring frequently, about 2 minutes, until the onions are softened. Add the sausage and cook, pressing with the back of a wooden spoon to break up the meat, 3–4 minutes, until the meat is no longer pink and the onions are golden.
2. Add the tomatoes, fennel seeds, salt and pepper; cook, stirring frequently, 10 minutes, until the vegetables are tender and the sauce is thickened.
3. Meanwhile, in a large pot of boiling water, cook the rigatoni according to package directions. Drain and place in a serving bowl. Add the sauce and cheese; toss to combine. Divide evenly among 4 plates and serve.

Serving (1¹/₂ cups) provides: 1 Fat, 3 Vegetables, ³/₄ Protein, 2 Breads, 5 Optional Calories.

Per Serving: 291 Calories, 9 g Total Fat, 1 g Saturated Fat, 24 mg Cholesterol, 394 mg Sodium, 41 g Total Carbohydrate, 3 g Dietary Fiber, 12 g Protein, 75 mg Calcium.

If fresh plum tomatoes are not available, substitute an equal number of chopped drained canned Italian plum tomatoes (no salt added).

SPAGHETTI WITH MEATBALLS

Perhaps the most popular Italian-American dish, this dynamic duo brings back many a childhood memory. Make a double batch of the sauce and freeze half for busy evenings.

Makes 8 servings

1 tablespoon + 1 teaspoon olive oil
1 medium onion, finely chopped
4 cups chopped drained canned
    Italian plum tomatoes (no salt
    added), juice reserved
1 garlic clove, minced
6 ounces lean ground beef
    (10% or less fat)
6 ounces lean ground veal
1 1/2 ounces Parmesan cheese, grated
3/4 cup minced fresh flat-leaf parsley
3 tablespoons plain dried bread
    crumbs

3 egg whites
1 tablespoon minced fresh basil
    (or 1 teaspoon dried)
2 teaspoons minced fresh oregano
    (or 1/2 teaspoon dried)
1 teaspoon minced fresh thyme
    leaves (or 1/4 teaspoon dried)
1/4 teaspoon salt
Freshly ground black pepper,
    to taste
12 ounces spaghetti
1 tablespoon + 1 teaspoon freshly
    grated Parmesan cheese (optional)

1. Place a large saucepan over medium heat 30 seconds; heat the oil 30 seconds more. Add the onion; cook, stirring frequently, about 2 minutes, until softened. Stir in the tomatoes and garlic; reduce the heat to medium-low and cook, stirring occasionally, about 5 minutes, until the mixture is bubbling.
2. In a large bowl, thoroughly combine the beef, veal, cheese, 1/4 cup of the parsley, the bread crumbs, egg whites, basil, oregano, thyme, salt and pepper.
3. Fill a medium bowl with cold water for moistening hands. With moistened hands, shape the meat mixture into 24 equal walnut-size meatballs. Drop the meatballs gently into the bubbling sauce.
4. Reduce the heat to low and simmer, without stirring, about 25 minutes, until the meatballs are cooked through and resistant to gentle pressure from a wooden spoon. Stir in the remaining 1/2 cup parsley; continue cooking, adding 1/4 cup reserved tomato juice at a time as needed, 30–45 minutes more, until the meatballs are tender and the sauce is thickened.

5. In a large pot of boiling water, cook the spaghetti according to package directions. Drain and place in a serving bowl. Add the sauce, meatballs and cheese (if using). Divide evenly among 8 plates and serve.

Serving (1 cup spaghetti with $^1/_4$ cup sauce and 3 meatballs, with optional Parmesan cheese) provides: $^1/_2$ Fat, 1 Vegetable, $1^1/_2$ Proteins, 2 Breads, 15 Optional Calories.

If optional Parmesan cheese is not used, reduce Optional Calories to 10.

Per Serving: 317 Calories, 8 g Total Fat, 3 g Saturated Fat, 35 mg Cholesterol, 264 mg Sodium, 41 g Total Carbohydrate, 3 g Dietary Fiber, 19 g Protein, 139 mg Calcium.

PAPPARDELLE WITH MEAT SAUCE

The Tuscans serve these wide ribbon noodles with a sauce of wild game. Turkey is a delicious substitute and makes a splendid counterpoint to the other savory ingredients; just be sure to leave enough time to marinate the turkey. A salad of wilted greens makes a pleasant side dish.

Makes 4 servings

10 ounces skinless boneless turkey thighs or drumsticks, cut into 1" chunks

4 fluid ounces (¹/₂ cup) dry red wine

1 rosemary sprig

1 tablespoon + 1 teaspoon olive oil

¹/₂ medium onion, chopped

1 celery stalk, chopped

¹/₄ cup chopped carrot

2 sun-dried tomato halves (not packed in oil), minced

1 garlic clove, minced

1 bay leaf

¹/₄ teaspoon salt

Freshly ground black pepper, to taste

1 tablespoon tomato paste (no salt added)

6 ounces pappardelle or other wide ribbon noodles

1 tablespoon + 1 teaspoon freshly grated Parmesan cheese

1. In a gallon-size sealable plastic bag, combine the turkey, wine and rosemary. Seal the bag, squeezing out air; turn to coat the turkey. Refrigerate at least 2 hours or overnight, turning the bag occasionally.

2. Drain the turkey; discard the rosemary, but reserve the wine. Place a medium nonstick saucepan over medium heat 30 seconds; heat the oil 30 seconds more. Add the turkey and reduce the heat to low; cook, stirring frequently, 5 minutes, until lightly browned. Add the onion, celery, carrot, tomato, garlic, bay leaf, salt and pepper; cook, stirring constantly, about 5 minutes, until the onion is golden.

3. Add 1 cup hot water, the reserved wine and the tomato paste and stir until the tomato paste is incorporated. Simmer, adding ¹/₄ cup water as needed, about 30 minutes, until the turkey is tender. Remove and discard the bay leaf. Transfer the turkey mixture to a food processor; pulse 3 or 4 times, until the meat is shredded.

4. Meanwhile, in a large pot of boiling water, cook the pappardelle according to package directions. Drain and place in a serving bowl. Add the sauce and cheese; toss to combine. Divide evenly among 4 plates and serve.

Serving (1^1/$_2$ cups) provides: 1 Fat, ^{3}/$_4$ Vegetable, 2 Proteins, 2 Breads, 35 Optional Calories.

Per serving: 337 Calories, 10 g Total Fat, 2 g Saturated Fat, 95 mg Total Cholesterol, 253 mg Sodium, 35 g Total Carbohydrate, 2 g Dietary Fiber, 22 g Protein, 71 mg Calcium.

RISOTTOS

RISOTTO WITH SWISS CHARD AND TOMATOES

All risottos have a wonderful blend of color, texture and taste, but in this one, the texture and colors are especially *magnifico*.

Makes 4 servings

$3^1/_2$ cups low-sodium vegetable broth

4 cups coarsely chopped well-washed trimmed Swiss chard (reserve stems)

1 tablespoon + 1 teaspoon olive oil

1 medium onion, finely chopped

4 large or 8 small plum tomatoes, peeled, seeded and chopped

7 ounces Arborio or other short-grain rice

8 fluid ounces (1 cup) dry white wine

1 tablespoon + 1 teaspoon freshly grated Parmesan cheese

Freshly ground black pepper, to taste

1. In a medium saucepan, bring the broth to a boil; reduce the heat and keep at a simmer.
2. In a large saucepan, bring 2" water to a boil. Arrange the Swiss chard leaves and stems on a steamer rack; place in the saucepan and cover with a tight-fitting lid. Steam 5 minutes, until barely tender.
3. Place another medium saucepan over medium heat 30 seconds; heat the oil 30 seconds more. Add the onion; cook, stirring frequently, 2 minutes, until softened. Add the tomatoes; cook 2 minutes, until they begin to release their juice.
4. Stir in the rice; cook, stirring constantly, 1 minute. Add the wine and $^1/_2$ cup of the broth; cook, stirring constantly, until all the liquid is absorbed. Stir in the Swiss chard. Continue adding the broth, $^1/_2$ cup at a time, stirring constantly until each addition is absorbed before adding more broth. The risotto should be done in 18–20 minutes, when the rice is tender and the mixture is creamy.
5. Remove from the heat; stir in the cheese and pepper. Divide evenly among 4 plates and serve at once.

Serving (1 cup) provides: 1 Fat, $3^1/_4$ Vegetables, $1^3/_4$ Breads, 80 Optional Calories.

Per Serving: 322 Calories, 6 g Total Fat, 1 g Saturated Fat, 2 mg Cholesterol, 186 mg Sodium, 51 g Total Carbohydrate, 2 g Dietary Fiber, 6 g Protein, 60 mg Calcium.

PUMPKIN RISOTTO

This sweet risotto is an excellent partner for poultry or pork. For a special touch, serve it in a pumpkin shell garnished with fresh sage.

Makes 4 servings

3$^1/_2$ cups low-sodium chicken broth

1 tablespoon + 1 teaspoon olive oil

2 medium onions, chopped

1 garlic clove, minced

7 ounces Arborio or other short-grain rice

8 fluid ounces (1 cup) dry white wine

1 cup pumpkin purée

1$^1/_2$ ounces Parmesan cheese, grated

$^1/_4$ teaspoon salt

Ground white pepper, to taste

$^1/_8$ teaspoon ground nutmeg

1. In a medium saucepan, bring the broth to a boil; reduce the heat and keep at a simmer.
2. Place another medium saucepan over medium heat 30 seconds; heat the oil 30 seconds more. Add the onions and garlic; cook, stirring frequently, 2 minutes, until softened.
3. Stir in the rice; cook, stirring constantly, 1 minute. Add the wine and $^1/_2$ cup of the broth and cook, stirring constantly, until all the liquid is absorbed. Continue adding the broth, $^1/_2$ cup at a time, stirring constantly, until each addition is absorbed before adding more broth. The risotto should be done in about 25 minutes, when the rice is tender and the mixture is creamy.
4. Reduce the heat to low. Stir in the pumpkin, cheese, salt and pepper; continue stirring until the mixture is warmed through. Sprinkle with the nutmeg. Divide evenly among 4 plates and serve at once.

Serving (1 cup) provides: 1 Fat, 1 Vegetable, $^1/_2$ Protein, 1$^3/_4$ Breads, 70 Optional Calories.

Per Serving: 357 Calories, 10 g Total Fat, 3 g Saturated Fat, 8 mg Cholesterol, 439 mg Sodium, 48 g Total Carbohydrate, 1 g Dietary Fiber, 11 g Protein, 187 mg Calcium.

RISOTTO WITH SPINACH AND GORGONZOLA CHEESE

Sharp Gorgonzola and slightly bitter spinach contrast wonderfully with the creamy texture of this elegant risotto. If you can't find Gorgonzola, substitute Roquefort, Stilton or another blue cheese.

Makes 4 servings

2 cups thawed frozen chopped spinach (one 10-ounce package)
3 cups low-sodium chicken broth
1 tablespoon + 1 teaspoon olive oil
2 medium onions, chopped
7 ounces Arborio or other short-grain rice

8 fluid ounces (1 cup) dry white wine
1 1/2 ounces Gorgonzola cheese, crumbled
Freshly ground black pepper, to taste

1. In a small saucepan, bring 1/2 cup of water to a boil; add spinach and cook according to package directions. Cover and set aside with the liquid.
2. In a medium saucepan, bring the broth to a boil; reduce the heat and keep at a simmer.
3. Place another medium saucepan over medium heat 30 seconds; heat the oil 30 seconds more. Add the onions; cook, stirring frequently, 2 minutes, until softened.
4. Stir in the rice; cook, stirring constantly, 1 minute. Add the wine and 1/2 cup of the broth; cook, stirring constantly, until all the liquid is absorbed. Stir in the spinach with its liquid. Continue adding the broth, 1/2 cup at a time, stirring constantly until each addition is absorbed before adding more broth. The risotto should be done in about 25 minutes, when the rice is tender and the mixture is creamy.
5. Remove from the heat; add the cheese and pepper, stirring vigorously until cheese is melted. Divide evenly among 4 plates and serve at once.

Serving (1 1/4 cups) provides: 1 Fat, 1 1/2 Vegetables, 1/2 Protein, 1 3/4 Breads, 65 Optional Calories.

Per Serving: 346 Calories, 10 g Total Fat, 4 g Saturated Fat, 9 mg Cholesterol, 289 mg Sodium, 47 g Total Carbohydrate, 3 g Dietary Fiber, 11 g Protein, 162 mg Calcium.

RISOTTO MILANESE

Saffron and lemon zest give this risotto its regal quality and lovely color. Its traditional partner is the braised veal shank dish, Osso Buco (page 128).

Makes 4 servings

$3^1/_2$ cups low-sodium chicken broth
$^1/_4$ teaspoon saffron threads
1 tablespoon olive oil
1 medium onion, chopped
7 ounces Arborio or other
   short-grain rice
4 fluid ounces ($^1/_2$ cup) dry white
   wine

$^3/_4$ ounce Parmesan cheese, grated
2 teaspoons reduced-calorie tub
   margarine
2 teaspoons grated lemon zest*
Freshly ground black or white
   pepper, to taste

1. In a medium saucepan, bring the broth to a boil; reduce the heat and keep at a simmer.
2. In a small bowl, dissolve the saffron in 1 cup of the broth.
3. Place another medium saucepan over medium heat 30 seconds; heat the oil 30 seconds more. Add the onion; cook, stirring frequently, 2 minutes, until softened.
4. Stir in the rice; cook, stirring constantly, 1 minute. Add the wine and $^1/_2$ cup of the broth and cook, stirring constantly, until all the liquid is absorbed. Continue adding the broth, alternating between plain broth and saffron broth, $^1/_2$ cup at a time, stirring constantly until each addition is absorbed before adding more broth. The risotto should be done in about 25 minutes, when the rice is tender and the mixture is creamy.
5. Remove from the heat; stir in the cheese, margarine, zest and pepper. Divide evenly among 4 plates and serve at once.

Serving (1 cup) provides: 1 Fat, $^1/_4$ Vegetable, $^1/_4$ Protein, $1^3/_4$ Breads, 45 Optional Calories.

Per Serving: 294 Calories, 9 g Total Fat, 2 g Saturated Fat, 4 mg Cholesterol, 216 mg Sodium, 43 g Total Carbohydrate, 1 g Dietary Fiber, 9 g Protein, 97 mg Calcium.

The zest of the lemon is the peel without any of the pith (white membrane). To remove zest from lemon, use a zester or the fine side of a vegetable grater; wrap lemon in plastic wrap and refrigerate for later use.

RISOTTO WITH RADICCHIO

Radicchio, the deep maroon, pleasantly bitter Italian lettuce, is delicious cooked. In this dish, it melts into the rice, and takes on a pretty magenta color as it mellows in flavor—a fascinating and delectable transformation.

Makes 4 servings

3¹/₂ cups low-sodium beef broth
1 tablespoon + 1 teaspoon olive oil
1 medium onion, chopped
7 ounces Arborio or other short-grain rice
1 medium head radicchio, trimmed and cut into ¹/₂" strips
8 fluid ounces (1 cup) dry red wine
³/₄ ounce Parmesan cheese, grated
Freshly ground black pepper, to taste

1. In a medium saucepan, bring the broth to a boil; reduce the heat and keep at a simmer.
2. Place another medium saucepan over medium heat 30 seconds; heat the oil 30 seconds more. Add the onion; cook, stirring frequently, 5 minutes, until golden.
3. Stir in the rice; cook, stirring constantly, 1 minute. Stir in the radicchio, wine and ¹/₂ cup of the broth and cook, stirring constantly, until all the liquid is absorbed. Continue adding the broth, ¹/₂ cup at a time, stirring constantly until each addition is absorbed before adding more broth. The risotto should be done in about 25 minutes, when the rice is tender and the mixture is creamy.
4. Remove from the heat; stir in the cheese and pepper. Divide evenly among 4 plates and serve at once.

Serving (1 cup) provides: 1 Fat, 1¹/₄ Vegetables, ¹/₄ Protein, 1³/₄ Breads, 70 Optional Calories.

Per Serving: 321 Calories, 6 g Total Fat, 2 g Saturated Fat, 4 mg Cholesterol, 169 mg Sodium, 45 g Total Carbohydrate, 2 g Dietary Fiber, 11 g Protein, 105 mg Calcium.

RISOTTO WITH FRESH HERBS

Whether your herb garden is a few pots on the window sill or a dedicated plot of land, this risotto is a perfect showcase for your green thumb. Experiment with different herbs and their flavors, but don't use any dried herbs—the taste just won't be the same.

Makes 4 servings

4$^1/_2$ cups low-sodium vegetable or
  chicken broth
2 tablespoons + 2 teaspoons
  reduced-calorie tub margarine
3 medium shallots, minced
8 medium scallions, thinly sliced
7 ounces Arborio or other
  short-grain rice

$^1/_2$ cup minced fresh parsley
$^1/_4$ cup minced fresh mint leaves
$^1/_4$ cup minced fresh chives
$^1/_4$ cup minced fresh basil
1 tablespoon + 1 teaspoon freshly
  grated Parmesan cheese
$^1/_4$ teaspoon ground white pepper

1. In a medium saucepan, bring the broth to a boil; reduce the heat and keep at a simmer.
2. Place another medium saucepan over medium-low heat 30 seconds; melt the margarine 30 seconds more. Add the shallots and scallions and cook, stirring frequently, 2 minutes, until the shallots are softened.
3. Stir in the rice; cook, stirring constantly, 1 minute. Raise the heat to medium; add 1$^1/_2$ cups of the broth and cook, stirring constantly, until all the liquid is absorbed. Continue adding the broth, $^1/_2$ cup at a time, stirring constantly until each addition is absorbed before adding more broth. The risotto should be done in about 25 minutes, when the rice is tender and the mixture is creamy.
4. Remove from the heat; stir in the parsley, mint, chives, basil, cheese and pepper. Divide evenly among 4 plates and serve at once.

Serving ($^3/_4$ cup) provides: 1 Fat, $^1/_2$ Vegetable, 1$^3/_4$ Breads, 35 Optional Calories.

Per Serving: 298 Calories, 7 g Total Fat, 1 g Saturated Fat, 2 mg Cholesterol, 184 mg Sodium, 53 g Total Carbohydrate, 1 g Dietary Fiber, 6 g Protein, 86 mg Calcium.

Risotto with Zucchini and Peppers

Red bell pepper and zucchini provide color, texture and a perfect example of how the Italians combine the best of the season and their pantry basics to create a masterpiece.

Makes 4 servings

4¹/₂ cups low-sodium vegetable broth
1 tablespoon + 1 teaspoon olive oil
2 medium onions, chopped
1 garlic clove, minced
7 ounces Arborio or other short-grain rice
4 medium zucchini, diced

1 medium red bell pepper, cored, seeded and diced
2 tablespoons minced fresh basil
2 tablespoons minced fresh oregano
1 tablespoon + 1 teaspoon freshly grated Parmesan cheese
Freshly ground black pepper, to taste

1. In a medium saucepan, bring the broth to a boil; reduce the heat and keep at a simmer.
2. Place another medium saucepan over medium-low heat 30 seconds; heat the oil 30 seconds more. Add the onions and garlic; cook, stirring frequently, 2 minutes, until softened.
3. Stir in the rice; cook, stirring constantly, 1 minute. Raise the heat to medium; add 1¹/₂ cups of the broth, the zucchini and bell pepper; cook, stirring constantly, until all the liquid is absorbed. Continue adding the broth, ¹/₂ cup at a time, stirring constantly until each addition is absorbed before adding more broth. The risotto should be done in about 25 minutes, when the rice and vegetables are tender and the mixture is creamy. Stir in the basil and oregano.
4. Remove from the heat; stir in the cheese and black pepper. Divide evenly among 4 plates and serve at once.

Serving (1 cup) provides: 1 Fat, 3 Vegetables, 1³/₄ Breads, 35 Optional Calories.

Per Serving: 314 Calories, 6 g Total Fat, 1 g Saturated Fat, 2 mg Cholesterol, 126 mg Sodium, 58 g Total Carbohydrate, 2 g Dietary Fiber, 8 g Protein, 87 mg Calcium.

RISOTTO WITH MUSHROOMS

Mushrooms lend an earthy quality to this classic northern Italian dish. Wild mushrooms such as porcini or shiitake make it even better—perfect with a roast or hearty meat dish.

Makes 4 servings

3^1/$_2$ cups low-sodium beef broth
1 tablespoon + 1 teaspoon olive oil
1 medium onion, chopped
3 medium shallots, minced
2 cups thinly sliced white
  mushrooms
2 cups thinly sliced shiitake or
  other wild mushrooms

7 ounces Arborio or other
  short-grain rice
8 ounces (1 cup) dry white wine
1 tablespoon + 1 teaspoon freshly
  grated Parmesan cheese
^{1}/$_4$ cup minced fresh flat-leaf parsley
Freshly ground black pepper,
  to taste

1. In a medium saucepan, bring the broth to a boil; reduce the heat and keep at a simmer.
2. Place another medium saucepan over medium-low heat 30 seconds; heat the oil 30 seconds more. Add the onion and shallots; cook, stirring frequently, 2 minutes, until softened. Add the mushrooms; cook, stirring frequently, 3 minutes, until they release some of their liquid.
3. Stir in the rice; cook, stirring constantly, 1 minute. Raise the heat to medium; add the wine and ^{1}/$_2$ cup of the broth; cook, stirring constantly, until all the liquid is absorbed. Continue adding the broth, ^{1}/$_2$ cup at a time, stirring constantly until each addition is absorbed before adding more broth. The risotto should be done in 18–20 minutes, when the rice and mushrooms are tender and the mixture is creamy.
4. Remove from the heat; stir in the parsley, cheese and pepper. Divide evenly among 4 plates and serve at once.

Serving (1 cup) provides: 1 Fat, 2^1/$_2$ Vegetables, 1^3/$_4$ Breads, 80 Optional Calories.

Per Serving: 326 Calories, 6 g Total Fat, 1 g Saturated Fat, 2 mg Cholesterol, 110 mg Sodium, 49 g Total Carbohydrate, 2 g Dietary Fiber, 11 g Protein, 55 mg Calcium.

RISOTTO WITH LEEKS AND FENNEL

The delicate licorice-like flavor of the fennel and the earthy flavor of the leeks join forces to make this a superb risotto. It goes beautifully with meat, fish or fowl, but is also hearty enough to stand by itself.

Makes 4 servings

$3^1/_2$ cups low-sodium vegetable broth

2 tablespoons + 2 teaspoons reduced-calorie tub margarine

2 cups thinly sliced well-washed trimmed leeks

2 medium fennel bulbs, chopped

7 ounces Arborio or other short-grain rice

8 fluid ounces (1 cup) dry white wine

$^3/_4$ ounce Parmesan cheese, grated

Freshly ground black pepper, to taste

1. In a medium saucepan, bring the broth to a boil; reduce the heat and keep at a simmer.
2. Place another medium saucepan over medium heat 30 seconds; melt 2 tablespoons of the margarine 30 seconds more. Add the leeks and fennel; cook, stirring frequently, 2 minutes, until the vegetables are softened.
3. Stir in the rice; cook, stirring constantly, 1 minute. Add the wine and $^1/_2$ cup of the broth; cook, stirring constantly, until all the liquid is absorbed. Continue adding the broth, $^1/_2$ cup at a time, stirring constantly until each addition is absorbed before adding more broth. The risotto should be done in about 25 minutes, when the rice and vegetables are tender and the mixture is creamy.
4. Remove from the heat; stir in remaining 2 teaspoons margarine, the cheese and pepper. Divide evenly among 4 plates and serve at once.

Serving (1 cup) provides: 1 Fat, 3 Vegetables, $^1/_4$ Protein, $1^3/_4$ Breads, 70 Optional Calories.

Per Serving: 367 Calories, 8 g Total Fat, 2 g Saturated Fat, 4 mg Cholesterol, 334 mg Sodium, 56 g Total Carbohydrate, 2 g Dietary Fiber, 8 g Protein, 161 mg Calcium.

RISOTTO WITH SHRIMP AND SCALLOPS

This is a truly elegant risotto—serve it with steamed fresh asparagus in the spring.

Makes 4 servings

$3^1/_2$ cups low-sodium chicken broth
1 tablespoon + 1 teaspoon olive oil
1 medium onion, chopped
7 ounces Arborio or other
  short-grain rice
8 fluid ounces (1 cup) dry white
  wine
10 ounces medium shrimp, peeled
  and deveined

10 ounces tiny bay scallops, rinsed
  and drained
1 tablespoon + 1 teaspoon freshly
  grated Parmesan cheese
1 tablespoon fresh thyme leaves
  (or 1 teaspoon dried leaves,
  crumbled)
Freshly ground black pepper,
  to taste

1. In a medium saucepan, bring the broth to a boil; reduce the heat and keep at a simmer.
2. Place another medium saucepan over medium heat 30 seconds; heat the oil 30 seconds more. Add the onion; cook, stirring frequently, 2 minutes, until softened.
3. Stir in the rice; cook, stirring constantly, 1 minute. Add the wine and $^1/_2$ cup of the broth; cook, stirring constantly, until all the liquid is absorbed. Continue adding the broth, $^1/_2$ cup at a time, stirring constantly until each addition is absorbed before adding more broth, until all but 1 cup of the broth has been used.
4. Add the remaining cup of broth, the shrimp and scallops; cook, stirring constantly, 6–8 minutes, until all the liquid is absorbed, the shrimp are pink, the scallops are just opaque and the mixture is creamy.
5. Remove from the heat; stir in the cheese, thyme and pepper. Divide evenly among 4 plates and serve at once.

Serving (1 cup) provides: 1 Fat, $^1/_4$ Vegetable, 2 Proteins, $1^3/_4$ Breads, 80 Optional Calories.

Per Serving: 420 Calories, 9 g Total Fat, 2 g Saturated Fat, 112 mg Cholesterol, 341 mg Sodium, 45 g Total Carbohydrate, 1 g Dietary Fiber, 31 g Protein, 107 mg Calcium.

6

FRITTATAS

FRITTATA WITH LEFTOVER SPAGHETTI

Purists may claim that leftover spaghetti is best cold, straight from the container, but Neapolitans recycle it into a delicious omelet that makes a great brunch or late supper. Add a salad or vegetable and you've got a meal.

Makes 4 servings

2 cups fat-free egg substitute
3 cups cooked spaghetti
1¹/₂ cups Tomato Sauce
   (page 20)

³/₄ ounce Parmesan cheese, grated
Freshly ground black pepper,
   to taste

1. Place the broiler rack 5" from heat. Preheat the broiler.
2. In a medium bowl, beat the egg substitute until frothy.
3. Spray the entire inside of a large nonstick skillet with a heatproof handle with nonstick cooking spray; place over medium heat 30 seconds. Pour the egg substitute into the skillet, tilting to cover the bottom of the pan. Arrange the spaghetti and pour the Tomato Sauce evenly over the egg substitute. Reduce the heat to low; cook 10–12 minutes, until the underside is set.
4. Broil the frittata 1–1¹/₂ minutes, until the top is set and a light crust is formed. Slide the frittata onto a large plate or platter; sprinkle evenly with the cheese and pepper. Cut into 4 equal wedges and serve.

Serving (1 wedge) provides: ³/₄ Fat, 1¹/₄ Vegetables, 1³/₄ Proteins, 1¹/₂ Breads.

Per Serving: 284 Calories, 6 g Total Fat, 2 g Saturated Fat, 4 mg Cholesterol, 411 mg Sodium, 37 g Total Carbohydrate, 3 g Dietary Fiber, 20 g Protein, 127 mg Calcium.

FRITTATA WITH PEPPERS AND POTATOES

Peppers and eggs have a natural affinity, and adding potatoes just makes a good thing better. For an extra treat, top this with a few spoonfuls of basic Tomato-Herb Sauce (page 21).

Makes 4 servings

1 tablespoon + 1 teaspoon olive oil
2 cups diced Italian frying peppers
10 ounces all-purpose potatoes,
   scrubbed and diced
2 cups fat-free egg substitute
1 tablespoon minced fresh oregano
   (or ¹/₂ teaspoon dried)

¹/₄ teaspoon salt
Freshly ground black pepper,
   to taste
2 teaspoons freshly grated
   Parmesan cheese

1. Place the broiler rack 5" from heat. Preheat the broiler.
2. Place a large nonstick skillet with a heatproof handle over medium heat 30 seconds; heat the oil 30 seconds more. Add the frying peppers, potatoes and 1 cup of hot water; cover and cook 15 minutes, stirring frequently and adding ¹/₂ cup water at a time as needed, until the vegetables are tender and the liquid is evaporated. Transfer to a bowl; set aside and keep warm.
3. In a medium bowl, combine the egg substitute, oregano, salt and pepper; beat until frothy.
4. Wipe out the skillet with a paper towel. Spray the entire inside of the skillet with nonstick cooking spray; place over medium heat 30 seconds. Pour the egg substitute mixture into the skillet, tilting to cover the bottom of the pan. Arrange the pepper mixture evenly over the egg substitute. Reduce the heat to low; cook 10–12 minutes, until the underside is set.
5. Broil the frittata 1–1¹/₂ minutes, until the top is set and a light crust is formed. Slide the frittata onto a large plate or platter; sprinkle evenly with the cheese. Cut into 4 equal wedges and serve.

Serving (1 wedge) provides: 1 Fat, 1 Vegetable, 1¹/₂ Proteins, ¹/₂ Bread, 5 Optional Calories.

Per Serving: 187 Calories, 5 g Total Fat, 1 g Saturated Fat, 1 mg Cholesterol, 364 mg Sodium, 21 g Total Carbohydrate, 2 g Dietary Fiber, 15 g Protein, 80 mg Calcium.

FRITTATA WITH POTATOES AND ONIONS

Frittatas are often eaten at room temperature, which makes them ideal make-aheads for weekend brunches or weekday lunches. And when they taste as good as this version, you'll find entertaining is a snap!

Makes 4 servings

2 tablespoons + 2 teaspoons reduced-calorie tub margarine
10 ounces pared all-purpose potatoes, scrubbed and diced
2 medium onions, chopped
2 cups fat-free egg substitute

$^1/_4$ cup minced fresh flat-leaf parsley
1 tablespoon + 1 teaspoon freshly grated Parmesan cheese
$^1/_4$ teaspoon salt
Freshly ground black pepper, to taste

1. Place the broiler rack 5" from heat. Preheat the broiler.
2. Place a large nonstick skillet with a heatproof handle over medium heat 30 seconds; melt the margarine 30 seconds more. Add the potatoes, onions and 1 cup of hot water; cook, stirring frequently and adding $^1/_2$ cup water at a time as needed, about 15 minutes, until the potatoes are golden, the onions are tender and the liquid is evaporated. Transfer to a medium bowl.
3. In another medium bowl, combine the egg substitute, parsley, cheese, salt and pepper; beat until frothy.
4. Wipe out the skillet with a paper towel. Spray the entire inside of the skillet with nonstick cooking spray; place over medium heat 30 seconds. Pour the egg substitute mixture into the skillet, tilting to cover the bottom of the pan. Arrange the potato mixture evenly over the egg substitute mixture. Reduce the heat to low and cook 10–12 minutes, until the underside is set.
5. Broil the frittata 1–1$^1/_2$ minutes, until the top is set and a light crust is formed. Slide the frittata onto a large plate or platter. Cut into 4 equal wedges and serve.

Serving (1 wedge) provides: 1 Fat, $^1/_2$ Vegetable, 1$^1/_2$ Proteins, $^1/_2$ Bread, 10 Optional Calories.

Per Serving: 186 Calories, 6 g Total Fat, 1 g Saturated Fat, 2 mg Cholesterol, 437 mg Sodium, 18 g Total Carbohydrate, 2 g Dietary Fiber, 15 g Protein, 91 mg Calcium.

FRITTATA WITH ARTICHOKE HEARTS AND MUSHROOMS

Artichoke hearts and mushrooms star in this frittata, which makes a wonderful dish for a spring brunch or luncheon.

Makes 4 servings

2 cups frozen artichoke hearts
  (one 10-ounce package)
1 tablespoon + 1 teaspoon olive oil
3 medium shallots, finely chopped
1 garlic clove, minced
2 cups sliced white mushrooms

2 cups fat-free egg substitute
$^{1}/_{4}$ cup minced fresh parsley
$^{3}/_{4}$ ounce Parmesan cheese, grated
$^{1}/_{4}$ teaspoon salt
Freshly ground black pepper,
  to taste

1. Place the broiler rack 5" from heat. Preheat the broiler.
2. Cook the artichoke hearts according to package directions, until tender. Cut into bite-size pieces and transfer to a medium bowl; set aside and keep warm.
3. Place a large nonstick skillet with a heatproof handle over medium heat 30 seconds; heat the oil 30 seconds more. Add the shallots and garlic; cook, stirring frequently, 2–3 minutes, until the shallots are softened. Stir in the mushrooms; cook about 5 minutes, until the mushrooms are tender and the shallots are light golden. Add to the artichokes.
4. In another medium bowl, beat the egg substitute until frothy.
5. Wipe out the skillet with a paper towel. Spray the entire inside of the skillet with nonstick cooking spray; place over medium heat 30 seconds. Pour the egg substitute into the skillet, tilting to cover the bottom of the pan. Arrange the mixture evenly over the egg substitute. Reduce the heat to low and cook 10–12 minutes, until the underside is set. Sprinkle with the parsley, cheese, salt and pepper.
6. Broil the frittata 1–1$^{1}/_{2}$ minutes, until the top is set and a light crust is formed. Slide the frittata onto a large plate or platter. Cut into 4 equal wedges and serve.

Serving (1 wedge) provides: 1 Fat, 2$^{1}/_{4}$ Vegetables, 1$^{3}/_{4}$ Proteins.

Per Serving: 179 Calories, 7 g Total Fat, 2 g Saturated Fat, 4 mg Cholesterol, 473 mg Sodium, 13 g Total Carbohydrate, 4 g Dietary Fiber, 17 g Protein, 143 mg Calcium.

Frittata with Zucchini, Peppers and Onions

Here's a super way to use up a bumper crop of zucchini and peppers.

Makes 4 servings

1 tablespoon + 1 teaspoon olive oil	$^1/_4$ cup minced fresh basil
2 medium onions, chopped	(or 2 teaspoons dried)
2 medium zucchini, diced	$^1/_4$ teaspoon salt
1 medium red or green bell pepper, diced	Freshly ground black pepper, to taste
2 cups fat-free egg substitute	$^3/_4$ ounce Parmesan cheese, grated

1. Place the broiler rack 5" from heat. Preheat the broiler.
2. Place a large nonstick skillet with a heatproof handle over medium heat 30 seconds; heat the oil 30 seconds more. Add the onions and cook, stirring frequently, 2 minutes, until softened. Add 2 cups of hot water, the zucchini and bell pepper; reduce the heat to medium-low, cover and cook, stirring frequently, 8 minutes, until the vegetables are tender. Uncover and cook 2–3 minutes, until the liquid is evaporated. Transfer the vegetables to a medium bowl; set aside and keep warm.
3. In a medium bowl, combine the egg substitute, basil, salt and pepper; beat until frothy.
4. Wipe out the skillet with a paper towel. Spray the entire inside of the skillet with nonstick cooking spray; place over medium heat 30 seconds. Pour the egg substitute mixture into the skillet, tilting to cover the bottom of the pan. Arrange the vegetables evenly over the egg substitute mixture. Reduce the heat to low and cook 10–12 minutes, until the underside is set.
5. Broil the frittata 1–1$^1/_2$ minutes, until the top is set and a light crust is formed. Slide the frittata onto a large plate or platter; sprinkle with the cheese. Cut into 4 equal wedges and serve.

Serving (1 wedge) provides: 1 Fat, 2 Vegetables, 1$^3/_4$ Proteins.

Per Serving: 160 Calories, 6 g Total Fat, 2 g Saturated Fat, 4 mg Cholesterol, 439 mg Sodium, 10 g Total Carbohydrate, 1 g Dietary Fiber, 16 g Protein, 153 mg Calcium.

FRITTATA WITH MOZZARELLA AND TOMATO SAUCE

This looks just like a pizza and it tastes just as good—maybe even better. With a crisp salad or vegetable antipasto, you've got a meal in minutes.

Makes 4 servings

2 cups fat-free egg substitute

³/₄ cup hot Tomato-Herb Sauce (page 21)

3 ounces skim-milk mozzarella cheese, shredded

Freshly ground black pepper, to taste

1. Place the broiler rack 5" from heat. Preheat the broiler.
2. In a medium bowl, beat the egg substitute until frothy.
3. Spray the entire inside of a large nonstick skillet with a heatproof handle with nonstick cooking spray; place over medium heat 30 seconds. Pour the egg substitute into the skillet, tilting to cover the bottom of the pan. Dot the surface with tablespoonsful of the Tomato-Herb Sauce; spread gently, but do not stir. Reduce the heat to low and cook 10–12 minutes, until the underside is set. Sprinkle with the cheese and pepper.
4. Broil the frittata 1–1¹/₂ minutes, until the top is set and the cheese is melted. Slide the frittata onto a large plate or platter. Cut into 4 equal wedges and serve.

Serving (1 wedge) provides: ¹/₂ Fat, ¹/₂ Vegetable, 2¹/₂ Proteins, 5 Optional Calories.

Per Serving: 119 Calories, 2 g Total Fat, 0 g Saturated Fat, 2 mg Cholesterol, 413 mg Sodium, 5 g Total Carbohydrate, 1 g Dietary Fiber, 19 g Protein, 201 mg Calcium.

RICE FRITTATA WITH FIGS AND PARMESAN CHEESE

This is a perfect fallback recipe when you can't get out to the grocery store, as it uses pantry staples. Be sure to keep the ingredients on hand for peace of mind.

Makes 4 servings

2 teaspoons olive oil	$^1/_2$ cup cooked white rice
1 medium onion, finely chopped	2 large dried figs, finely chopped
$^1/_2$ small garlic clove, minced	$^3/_4$ ounce Parmesan cheese, grated
1 cup fat-free egg substitute	$^1/_4$ teaspoon dried thyme

1. Place the broiler rack 5" from heat. Preheat the broiler.
2. Place a medium nonstick saucepan with a heatproof handle over medium heat 30 seconds; heat the oil 30 seconds more. Add the onion and garlic; cook, stirring frequently, 2 minutes, until softened.
3. In a large bowl, beat the egg substitute until frothy; stir in the onion mixture, rice, figs, cheese and thyme.
4. Wipe out the skillet with a paper towel. Spray the entire inside of the skillet with nonstick cooking spray; place over medium heat 30 seconds. Pour the egg substitute mixture into the skillet, tilting to cover the bottom of the pan. Reduce the heat to low and cook 10–12 minutes, until the underside is set.
5. Broil the frittata 1–1$^1/_2$ minutes, until the top is set and a light crust is formed. Slide the frittata onto a large plate or platter. Cut into 4 equal wedges and serve.

Serving (1 wedge) provides: $^1/_2$ Fat, $^1/_2$ Fruit, $^1/_4$ Vegetable, 1 Protein, $^1/_4$ Bread.

Per Serving: 145 Calories, 4 g Total Fat, 1 g Saturated Fat, 4 mg Cholesterol, 201 mg Sodium, 17 g Total Carbohydrate, 1 g Dietary Fiber, 9 g Protein, 118 mg Calcium.

7

SALADS

Cauliflower, Celery and Olive Salad

Tricolor Salad of Radicchio, Endive and Arugula

Arugula and Radicchio Salad with Balsamic Vinegar and Crumbled Parmesan Cheese

Arugula and Potato Salad

Wilted Swiss Chard and Spinach Salad

Panzanella

White Bean and Sage Salad

Lentil Salad

Chick-Pea and Rosemary Salad

CAULIFLOWER, CELERY AND OLIVE SALAD

Traditionally a Neapolitan Christmas dish, this is a salad for all seasons.

Makes 4 servings

6 cups bite-size cauliflower florets
2 medium celery stalks, chopped
10 pitted small green olives
10 pitted small black olives
1/2 cup chopped pickled sweet red peppers
1 tablespoon rinsed drained capers
1 tablespoon + 1 teaspoon extra virgin olive oil

1 tablespoon cider vinegar
2 tablespoons low-sodium vegetable broth
1/4 teaspoon salt
Freshly ground black pepper, to taste
Fresh minced parsley, to garnish

1. In a large saucepan, bring 2" water to a boil. Arrange the cauliflower on a steamer rack; place in the saucepan and cover with a tight-fitting lid. Steam 5–7 minutes, until tender-crisp. Cool under running water; drain and set aside.

2. In a medium bowl, combine the celery, green and black olives, red peppers, capers, oil, vinegar, broth, salt and black pepper. Add the cauliflower; toss well. Cover and refrigerate 6–8 hours or overnight.

3. Remove from the refrigerator and bring to room temperature; toss gently. Divide evenly among 4 plates and serve, garnished with the parsley.

Serving (2 cups) provides: 1 1/2 Fats, 3 1/2 Vegetables.

Per Serving: 102 Calories, 7 g Total Fat, 1 g Saturated Fat, 0 mg Cholesterol, 496 mg Sodium, 10 g Total Carbohydrate, 4 g Dietary Fiber, 3 g Protein, 61 mg Calcium.

TRICOLOR SALAD OF RADICCHIO, ENDIVE AND ARUGULA

A refreshing mixture of tangy and bitter greens, this salad makes a colorful addition to just about any menu.

Makes 4 servings

1 medium head radicchio
1 medium bunch arugula
1 head Belgian endive

¹/₄ cup Oil and Vinegar Salad Dressing (page 18)

1. Remove the tough outer leaves from the radicchio; discard. Pull off the remaining leaves; set aside 8 of the largest ones. Tear the remaining leaves into bite-size pieces. Wash all the leaves in cold water; pat dry with paper towels.
2. Remove the stems and discolored leaves from the arugula; discard. Wash in cold water; pat dry with paper towels. Tear into bite-size pieces.
3. Separate the leaves of the Belgian endive. Wash in cold water; pat dry with paper towels. Reserve 12 of the largest leaves; cut the remaining leaves into 1" slices.
4. On each of 4 salad plates, arrange 2 of the whole radicchio leaves and 3 of the endive leaves in a petal pattern. In a large bowl, toss the remaining radicchio, endive and arugula with the dressing. Place one-fourth of the salad in the center of each plate; serve at once.

Serving (1¹/₄ cups) provides: 1 Fat, 2¹/₄ Vegetables, 10 Optional Calories.

Per Serving: 69 Calories, 5 g Total Fat, 1 g Saturated Fat, 0 mg Cholesterol, 159 mg Sodium, 4 g Total Carbohydrate, 2 g Dietary Fiber, 2 g Protein, 77 mg Calcium.

ARUGULA AND RADICCHIO SALAD WITH BALSAMIC VINEGAR AND CRUMBLED PARMESAN CHEESE

It's amazing how some of the best salads are the simplest ones. Balsamic vinegar enhances the flavor of this salad, and cheese provides a tasty complement.

Makes 4 Servings

1 medium head radicchio
1 medium bunch arugula
2 tablespoons balsamic vinegar
2 teaspoons extra virgin olive oil

1 1/2 ounces Parmesan cheese, crumbled
Freshly ground black pepper, to taste

1. Remove the tough outer leaves from the radicchio and trim a thin slice from the bottom of the core; discard. Pull off the remaining leaves, wash in cold water; pat dry with paper towels.
2. Remove the stems and discolored leaves from the arugula; discard. Wash the remaining leaves in cold water; pat dry with paper towels.
3. Divide the radicchio leaves evenly among 4 plates; pile the arugula leaves evenly in the center of each.
4. Drizzle evenly with the vinegar and oil. Sprinkle evenly with cheese, then pepper. Serve at once.

Serving (1 cup) provides: 1/2 Fat, 2 Vegetables, 1/2 Protein.

Per Serving: 79 Calories, 6 g Total Fat, 2 g Saturated Fat, 8 mg Total Cholesterol, 218 mg Sodium, 2 g Total Carbohydrate, 1 g Dietary Fiber, 6 g Protein, 217 mg Calcium.

ARUGULA AND POTATO SALAD

New potatoes in a light dressing combined with peppery arugula are a far cry from our American mayonnaise-based concept of potato salad. If you can't find arugula, use watercress.

Makes 4 servings

1 pound 4 ounces pared new
  potatoes
1 medium bunch arugula
4 medium scallions, sliced
1 fluid ounce (2 tablespoons) dry
  white wine
1 tablespoon + 1 teaspoon extra
  virgin olive oil

1 tablespoon white wine vinegar
1 garlic clove, bruised
$1/4$ teaspoon salt
Freshly ground black pepper,
  to taste

1. Place the potatoes in a medium saucepan; add cold water to cover. Cover the pan with a lid and bring to a boil; reduce the heat to low and simmer 20 minutes, until tender. Drain and set aside.
2. Meanwhile, remove the stems and discolored leaves from the arugula; discard. Wash in cold water; pat dry with paper towels. Place one-fourth around the edges of each of 4 plates; set aside.
3. In a large bowl, whisk together the scallions, wine, oil, vinegar, garlic, salt and pepper. Cut the potatoes into $1/2$" slices; while still warm, add to the dressing and toss to coat thoroughly.
4. Just before serving, remove the garlic; place one-fourth of the potato salad in the center of each plate. Serve warm or at room temperature, but not cold.

Serving (2 cups) provides: 1 Fat, 1 Vegetable, 1 Bread, 5 Optional Calories.

Per Serving: 168 Calories, 5 g Total Fat, 1 g Saturated Fat, 0 mg Cholesterol, 165 mg Sodium, 27 g Total Carbohydrate, 4 g Dietary Fiber, 4 g Protein, 59 mg Calcium.

WILTED SWISS CHARD AND SPINACH SALAD

Italian cooks know how to coax the flavor out of the simplest foods. Dressed with olive oil and lemon juice, cooked greens are particularly welcome with most meat-, fish- and cheese-based dishes.

Makes 4 servings

4 cups coarsely chopped trimmed Swiss chard (reserve the stems)
4 cups coarsely chopped trimmed spinach
1 tablespoon fresh lemon juice

2 teaspoons extra virgin olive oil
¼ teaspoon salt
Freshly ground black pepper, to taste

1. Cut the thin, tender Swiss chard stems into 1" pieces; discard the thick, tough stems. Wash the Swiss chard and spinach thoroughly; do not dry them.
2. Place the Swiss chard leaves and stems and the spinach leaves in a large saucepan; cook with only the water that clings to them, stirring occasionally and adding 1 tablespoon water at a time as needed, 10 minutes, until the leaves are wilted and the stems are tender.
3. Drain and squeeze out any excess moisture; place in a serving bowl. While still warm, drizzle with the lemon juice, oil, salt and pepper. Divide evenly among 4 plates and serve warm or at room temperature.

Serving (½ cup) provides: ½ Fat, 4 Vegetables.

Per Serving: 40 Calories, 3 g Total Fat, 0 g Saturated Fat, 0 mg Cholesterol, 256 mg Sodium, 4 g Total Carbohydrate, 2 g Dietary Fiber, 2 g Protein, 75 mg Calcium.

PANZANELLA

BREAD AND TOMATO SALAD

The Tuscans are equally proud of their crusty bread and their frugality. This savory salad puts both to good use; it's perfect for days when the garden is brimming and the bread a day or so old. For best results, use only ripe, in-season tomatoes.

Makes 4 servings

8 ounces 1- or 2-day-old crusty Italian bread, coarsely chopped

4 medium tomatoes, peeled and chopped

4 medium celery stalks, finely chopped

2 medium red onions, chopped

$^1/_2$ cup minced fresh parsley

2 tablespoons red wine vinegar

1 tablespoon + 1 teaspoon extra virgin olive oil

2 garlic cloves, minced

$^1/_4$ teaspoon salt

$^1/_4$ teaspoon freshly ground black pepper

$^1/_4$ cup minced fresh basil

1. In a medium bowl, soak the bread in water for 3 minutes, until soggy. Drain and squeeze dry; discard water. Return the bread to the bowl. Using a fork, break it into small pieces.
2. In a large bowl, combine the tomatoes, celery, onions, parsley, vinegar, oil, garlic, salt and pepper. Let stand for 30 minutes, until the tomatoes have released some of their juice.
3. Stir the bread into the tomato mixture; sprinkle with the basil. Divide evenly among 4 plates and serve at room temperature.

Serving (2 cups) provides: 1 Fat, 3 Vegetables, 2 Breads.

Per Serving: 257 Calories, 7 g Total Fat, 1 g Saturated Fat, 0 mg Cholesterol, 514 mg Sodium, 43 g Total Carbohydrate, 5 g Dietary Fiber, 8 g Protein, 114 mg Calcium.

WHITE BEAN AND SAGE SALAD

You won't go very far in Tuscany without encountering beans and sage. This salad is delicious as is, or enhanced with red onion, canned tuna, or both. It's also a terrific source of protein and fiber.

Makes 4 servings

2 tablespoons minced fresh sage leaves (or 2 teaspoons dried)
1 tablespoon + 1 teaspoon extra virgin olive oil
1 tablespoon dry white wine
1 tablespoon white wine vinegar

2 garlic cloves, minced
$^{1}/_{4}$ teaspoon salt
Freshly ground black pepper, to taste
1 pound drained cooked cannellini (white kidney) beans

In a large bowl, whisk together the sage, oil, wine, vinegar, garlic, salt and pepper. Add the beans; toss to coat thoroughly. Cover and let stand 1–2 hours. Divide evenly among 4 plates and serve.

Serving ($^{1}/_{2}$ cup) provides: 1 Fat, 2 Proteins, 5 Optional Calories.

Per Serving: 190 Calories, 5 g Total Fat, 1 g Saturated Fat, 0 mg Cholesterol, 138 mg Sodium, 27 g Total Carbohydrate, 4 g Dietary Fiber, 10 g Protein, 41 mg Calcium.

LENTIL SALAD

Because lentils are said to bring financial luck, they are traditionally served in Italy on New Year's Day.

Makes 4 servings

6 ounces lentils, rinsed and drained
2 garlic cloves, bruised
1 bay leaf
1 medium carrot, diced
3 medium celery stalks, diced
1 medium onion, diced
$^1/_2$ medium green bell pepper, seeded and diced
$^1/_4$ cup minced fresh mint leaves
$^1/_4$ cup minced fresh parsley

2 fluid ounces ($^1/_4$ cup) dry white wine
1 tablespoon + 1 teaspoon extra virgin olive oil
1 tablespoon + 1 teaspoon white wine vinegar
$^1/_4$ teaspoon salt
Freshly ground black pepper, to taste

1. In a medium saucepan, combine 6 cups of water with the lentils, garlic and bay leaf. Bring to a boil over low heat; cover and cook about 15 minutes, until lentils are tender but firm. Rinse and drain the lentils; discard the garlic and bay leaf.
2. In a large bowl, combine the carrot, celery, onion, bell pepper, mint, parsley, wine, oil, vinegar, salt and pepper. Add the lentils; toss to coat thoroughly. Cover and let stand until slightly warm or at room temperature; do not refrigerate. Divide evenly among 4 plates and serve.

Serving (1 cup) provides: 1 Fat, 1$^1/_2$ Vegetables, 2 Proteins, 15 Optional Calories.

Per Serving: 224 Calories, 5 g Total Fat, 1 g Saturated Fat, 0 mg Cholesterol, 171 mg Sodium, 31 g Total Carbohydrate, 7 g Dietary Fiber, 13 g Protein, 56 mg Calcium.

CHICK-PEA AND ROSEMARY SALAD

The rich texture of the chick-peas cuts through the almost astringent taste of rosemary in this refreshing salad.

Makes 4 servings

2 large plum tomatoes, peeled, seeded and finely chopped

3 tablespoons minced fresh rosemary leaves (or 1¹/₂ teaspoons dried)

1 tablespoon + 1 teaspoon extra virgin olive oil

1 tablespoon + 1 teaspoon white wine vinegar

1 garlic clove, minced

¹/₄ teaspoon salt

Freshly ground black pepper, to taste

1 pound drained cooked chick-peas

In a large bowl, combine the tomatoes, rosemary, oil, vinegar, garlic, salt and pepper. Let stand 30 minutes, until the flavors are blended. Add the chick-peas; toss to coat thoroughly. Let stand 30 minutes more, until the chick-peas have absorbed the flavors; do not refrigerate. Divide evenly among 4 plates and serve.

Serving (¹/₂ cup) provides: 1 Fat, ¹/₂ Vegetable, 2 Proteins.

Per Serving: 235 Calories, 8 g Total Fat, 1 g Saturated Fat, 0 mg Cholesterol, 146 mg Sodium, 33 g Total Carbohydrate, 4 g Dietary Fiber, 10 g Protein, 64 mg Calcium.

8

FISH AND SEAFOOD

Shrimp in Marinara Sauce

Baked Flounder with Lemon, Parsley and Bread Crumbs

Baked Striped Bass with Shrimp and Clams

Grilled Red Snapper with Herb Pesto

Seared Tuna with Onions and Anchovies

Broiled Tuna with Fennel-Crumb Crust

Grilled Swordfish and Summer Vegetable Kabobs

Broiled Swordfish with Anchovy-Crumb Crust

SHRIMP IN MARINARA SAUCE

Alone or with pasta, this dish is quick, easy and delicious—it's the perfect recipe to turn to when you need last-minute company or family fare.

Makes 4 servings

1 tablespoon + 1 teaspoon olive oil

1 pound 4 ounces large shrimp, peeled and deveined

2 garlic cloves, minced

1 cup drained canned plum tomatoes (no salt added)

8 fluid ounces (1 cup) dry white wine

2 tablespoons minced fresh flat-leaf parsley

2 tablespoons tomato paste (no salt added)

1 tablespoon minced fresh oregano (or ¹/₂ teaspoon dried)

¹/₄ teaspoon salt

¹/₄ teaspoon crushed red pepper flakes

1. Place a large nonstick skillet over medium heat 30 seconds; heat the oil 30 seconds more. Add the shrimp and garlic; cook, stirring constantly, 3 minutes, until the shrimp are pink.

2. Stir in the tomatoes, wine, parsley, tomato paste, oregano, salt and pepper flakes. Bring to a boil; cook stirring frequently, 8 minutes, until the sauce is thickened. Divide evenly among 4 plates and serve at once.

Serving (4 ounces shrimp with 2 tablespoons sauce) provides: 1 Fat, ³/₄ Vegetable, 2 Proteins, 50 Optional Calories.

Per Serving: 224 Calories, 7 g Total Fat, 1 g Saturated Fat, 174 mg Cholesterol, 322 mg Sodium, 6 g Total Carbohydrate, 1 g Dietary Fiber, 24 g Protein, 93 mg Calcium.

BAKED FLOUNDER WITH LEMON, PARSLEY AND BREAD CRUMBS

Use the freshest fish you can find. Besides flounder or sole, red snapper, catfish, and trout are also good choices.

Makes 4 servings

15 ounces flounder or sole fillets,
   cut into 4 equal pieces
$^1/_4$ cup fresh lemon juice
4 teaspoons olive oil
3 tablespoons + 2 teaspoons plain
   dried bread crumbs

$^1/_4$ teaspoon salt
$^1/_4$ teaspoon ground white pepper
$^1/_2$ cup minced fresh flat-leaf parsley
Fresh lemon wedges and flat-leaf
   parsley sprigs, to garnish

1. Preheat the oven to 350° F. Spray a 13 × 9" baking dish with nonstick cooking spray.
2. Place the fillets, skin-side down, in the baking dish. Sprinkle them evenly with the lemon juice. Brush each fillet with 1 teaspoon oil.
3. In a small bowl, combine the bread crumbs, salt and pepper; sprinkle evenly over the fillets.
4. Bake the fillets 15 minutes, until the fish is opaque and flakes easily when tested with a fork. Place one fillet on each of 4 plates and sprinkle with minced parsley. Serve garnished with lemon wedges and parsley sprigs.

Serving (3 ounces fish) provides: 1 Fat, $1^1/_2$ Proteins, $^1/_4$ Bread, 5 Optional Calories.

Per Serving: 170 Calories, 6 g Total Fat, 1 g Saturated Fat, 51 mg Cholesterol, 278 mg Sodium, 6 g Total Carbohydrate, 1 g Dietary Fiber, 21 g Protein, 45 mg Calcium.

BAKED STRIPED BASS WITH SHRIMP AND CLAMS

All the tastes of the deep blue sea come together in this elegant, easy and attractive dish. Although we like striped bass in this, any firm-fleshed non-oily fillet will do; let what's fresh at the market dictate your choice.

Makes 4 servings

15 ounces striped bass fillet
5 ounces medium shrimp, peeled and deveined
12 small clams, scrubbed
2 fluid ounces ($^1/_4$ cup) dry white wine
2 tablespoons minced fresh parsley

2 tablespoons fresh lemon juice
2 teaspoons olive oil
$^1/_4$ teaspoon salt
Freshly ground black pepper, to taste
1 lemon, cut into 8 slices
4 fresh thyme sprigs

1. Preheat the oven to 400° F. Spray a 13 × 9" baking dish with nonstick cooking spray.
2. Arrange the fish, shrimp and clams in the baking dish.
3. In a small bowl, combine the wine, parsley, juice, oil, salt and pepper; drizzle the mixture evenly over the fish and shellfish. Top with the lemon slices and thyme sprigs. Cover with foil and bake 20 minutes, until the fish flakes easily when tested with a fork, the shrimp are pink and the unopened clams open. Discard any unopened clams. Divide evenly among 4 plates and serve at once.

Serving (3 ounces bass, 1 ounce shrimp and 3 clams with $^1/_4$ of the cooking liquid) provides: $^1/_2$ Fat, $2^1/_2$ Proteins, 15 Optional Calories.

Per Serving: 194 Calories, 6 g Total Fat, 1 g Saturated Fat, 138 mg Cholesterol, 269 mg Sodium, 5 g Total Carbohydrate, 0 g Dietary Fiber, 29 g Protein, 50 mg Calcium.

GRILLED RED SNAPPER WITH HERB PESTO

Marinating and grilling really bring out the flavors of fish, and a concentrated herb pesto enhances it even more. If you can't find red snapper, try trout, flounder, sole, or any non-oily fish fillet.

Makes 4 servings

$^1/_4$ cup fresh lemon juice

2 fluid ounces ($^1/_4$ cup) dry white wine

2 rinsed drained anchovy fillets, chopped (or 1 teaspoon anchovy paste)

15 ounces red snapper fillets

1 cup packed fresh basil leaves

$^1/_2$ cup packed fresh parsley leaves

$^1/_2$ cup packed fresh mint leaves

1 tablespoon + 1 teaspoon olive oil

2 garlic cloves

$^1/_4$ teaspoon salt

Freshly ground black pepper, to taste

1. To prepare the marinade, in a gallon-size sealable plastic bag, combine the juice, wine and anchovies; add the fish. Seal the bag, squeezing out air; turn to coat the fish. Refrigerate at least 2 hours or overnight, turning the bag occasionally.
2. Spray the broiler or grill rack with nonstick cooking spray; place 5" from heat. Preheat the broiler, or prepare the grill according to the manufacturer's instructions.
3. Meanwhile, in a food processor or blender, combine the basil, parsley, mint, oil, garlic, salt and pepper; purée until smooth. Transfer to a small bowl.
4. Broil or grill the fish 10 minutes. Spread the herb mixture evenly over the fish; cook 2 minutes more, until the fish flakes easily when tested with a fork and the pesto is heated through. Divide evenly among 4 plates and serve at once.

Serving (3 ounces red snapper with 1 tablespoon pesto) provides: 1 Fat, $1^1/_2$ Proteins, 15 Optional Calories.

Per Serving: 189 Calories, 6 g Total Fat, 1 g Saturated Fat, 40 mg Cholesterol, 284 mg Sodium, 7 g Total Carbohydrate, 1 g Dietary Fiber, 24 g Protein, 210 mg Calcium.

SEARED TUNA WITH ONIONS AND ANCHOVIES

Although this recipe calls for cooking the fish just until rare, feel free to make it as well done as you like.

Makes 4 servings

2 medium onions, thinly sliced
4 fluid ounces ($^1/_2$ cup) dry white
   wine
2 garlic cloves, minced
2 teaspoons olive oil
Four 5-ounce tuna steaks, 1" thick
2 large or 4 small plum tomatoes,
   peeled, seeded and chopped*

$^1/_4$ cup chopped fresh flat-leaf
   parsley
1 tablespoon white wine vinegar
4 rinsed drained anchovy fillets,
   chopped (or 2 teaspoons
   anchovy paste)
$^1/_2$ teaspoon crushed red pepper
   flakes

1. Spray a medium nonstick skillet with nonstick cooking spray; place over medium heat 30 seconds. Add the onions, wine and garlic; cook, stirring frequently, 5 minutes, until the onions are transparent. Remove from the heat; cover and set aside to keep warm.
2. Place another medium nonstick skillet over medium heat 30 seconds; heat the oil 30 seconds more. Add the tuna; cook 1–1$^1/_2$ minutes; turn and cook 1$^1/_2$ minutes more, or to desired doneness.
3. As soon as the tuna is turned, put the skillet with the onions back over medium heat. Uncover and add the tomatoes, parsley, vinegar, anchovies and pepper flakes; cook, stirring constantly, 12 minutes, until heated through.
4. Transfer the tuna steaks to a warmed serving platter; pour the sauce evenly over them. Serve at once.

Serving (4 ounces tuna with $^1/_4$ cup sauce) provides: $^1/_2$ Fat, 1 Vegetable, 2 Proteins, 35 Optional Calories.

Per Serving: 279 Calories, 10 g Total Fat, 2 g Saturated Fat, 56 mg Cholesterol, 209 mg Sodium, 6 g Total Carbohydrate, 1 g Dietary Fiber, 35 g Protein, 30 mg Calcium.

If fresh plum tomatoes are not available, substitute an equal number of chopped drained canned Italian plum tomatoes (no salt added).

BROILED TUNA WITH FENNEL-CRUMB CRUST

The fresh taste of fennel will perk up this or any fish.

Makes 4 servings

3 tablespoons plain dried bread crumbs
2 tablespoons minced fennel bulb
1 tablespoon fresh lemon juice
1 tablespoon minced fresh parsley

2 teaspoons olive oil
1 teaspoon fennel seeds, crushed
$^1/_4$ teaspoon salt
$^1/_4$ teaspoon ground white pepper
Four 4-ounce tuna steaks

1. Spray the broiler rack with nonstick cooking spray; place 5" from heat. Preheat the broiler.
2. In a small bowl, combine the bread crumbs, minced fennel, juice, parsley, oil, fennel seeds, salt and pepper.
3. Broil the fish 5 minutes; turn and broil 3 minutes more. Spread the bread crumb mixture evenly over the tuna; broil 3 minutes, until the fish flakes easily when tested with a fork and the crust is a deep gold. Place one tuna steak on each of 4 plates and serve at once.

Serving (3 ounces tuna with crust) provides: $^1/_2$ Fat, $1^1/_2$ Proteins, $^1/_4$ Bread.

Per Serving: 207 Calories, 8 g Total Fat, 2 g Saturated Fat, 43 mg Cholesterol, 227 mg Sodium, 4 g Total Carbohydrate, 0 g Dietary Fiber, 27 g Protein, 22 mg Calcium.

GRILLED SWORDFISH AND SUMMER VEGETABLE KABOBS

Spiedini, skewers of flavorful swordfish and colorful summer vegetables, are marinated with pungent herbs, then grilled to make picture-perfect barbecue fare. Get everything ready ahead of time, then grill at the last minute.

Makes 4 servings

8 fluid ounces (1 cup) dry white wine

¹/₄ cup fresh lemon juice

2 tablespoons minced fresh rosemary leaves (or 1 teaspoon dried)

2 tablespoons minced fresh oregano (or 1 teaspoon dried)

1 tablespoon minced fresh thyme leaves (or ¹/₂ teaspoon dried)

2 teaspoons olive oil

2 garlic cloves, minced

2 rinsed drained anchovy fillets, chopped (or 1 teaspoon anchovy paste)

Freshly ground black pepper, to taste

1 pound 4 ounces swordfish steak, cut into 1" cubes

1 medium green bell pepper, cut into 1" pieces

1 medium red or yellow bell pepper, cut into 1" pieces

8 large plum tomatoes, halved and seeded

2 medium zucchini, cut into 1" slices

1 large onion, cut into 8 wedges

1. To prepare the marinade, in a gallon-size sealable plastic bag, combine the wine, juice, rosemary, oregano, thyme, oil, garlic, anchovies and black pepper; add the fish, bell peppers, tomatoes, zucchini and onion. Seal the bag, squeezing out air; turn to coat the fish and vegetables thoroughly. Refrigerate at least 2 hours or overnight, turning the bag occasionally.

2. Spray the broiler rack or grill with nonstick cooking spray; place 5" from heat. Preheat the broiler, or prepare the grill according to the manufacturer's instructions. Prepare eight 18" or longer skewers: If using wooden skewers, soak in water at least 15 minutes; if using metal skewers, spray with nonstick cooking spray.

3. Drain the marinade into a small saucepan and bring to a rolling boil; boil for 1 minute, stirring constantly. Remove from the heat.

4. Alternating the ingredients and dividing them evenly, thread the fish and vegetables onto the skewers. Place the skewers on the prepared grill or broiler rack; baste with half the marinade.

5. Grill or broil the kabobs 5 minutes, until brown. Turn and baste with the remaining marinade; cook 5 minutes more, until the fish flakes easily when tested with a fork and the vegetables are slightly charred. Place 2 kabobs on each of 4 plates and serve at once.

Serving (4 ounces swordfish with 2$^1/_4$ cups vegetables) provides: $^1/_2$ Fat, 4$^1/_4$ Vegetables, 2 Proteins, 55 Optional Calories.

Per Serving: 307 Calories, 9 g Total Fat, 2 g Saturated Fat, 56 mg Cholesterol, 219 mg Sodium, 17 g Total Carbohydrate, 3 g Dietary Fiber, 32 g Protein, 63 mg Calcium.

Broiled Swordfish with Anchovy-Crumb Crust

Anchovies figure largely in Italian cooking. Here they pair up with bread crumbs and capers to form a savory topping for fresh swordfish. This crust is great on mako and tuna, too.

Makes 4 servings

$^1/_3$ cup + 2 teaspoons plain dried bread crumbs

2 fluid ounces ($^1/_4$ cup) dry white wine

1 teaspoon grated lemon zest*

2 tablespoons fresh lemon juice

1 tablespoon minced fresh oregano (or $^1/_2$ teaspoon dried)

1 tablespoon rinsed drained capers

2 teaspoons olive oil

2 rinsed drained anchovy fillets, chopped (or 1 teaspoon anchovy paste)

Freshly ground black pepper, to taste

One 15-ounce swordfish steak, 1" thick

1. Spray the broiler rack with nonstick cooking spray; place 5" from heat. Preheat the broiler.
2. In a food processor, combine the bread crumbs, wine, zest, juice, oregano, capers, oil, anchovies and pepper. Pulse until thoroughly combined.
3. Broil the fish 5 minutes; turn and broil 2 minutes more. Spread the crumb mixture evenly over the fish; broil 3–4 minutes, until the fish flakes easily when tested with a fork and the crust is a deep gold. Divide evenly among 4 plates and serve at once.

Serving (3 ounces swordfish with crust) provides: $^1/_2$ Fat, $1^1/_2$ Proteins, $^1/_2$ Bread, 15 Optional Calories.

Per Serving: 206 Calories, 7 g Total Fat, 2 g Saturated Fat, 43 mg Cholesterol, 312 mg Sodium, 8 g Total Carbohydrate, 0 g Dietary Fiber, 23 g Protein, 37 mg Calcium.

*The zest of the lemon is the peel without any of the pith (white membrane). To remove zest from lemon, use a zester or the fine side of a vegetable grater.

POULTRY
AND MEATS

Chicken Marsala

Roasted Chicken with Potatoes and Onions

Beef-Stuffed Frying Peppers

Grilled Sirloin with Fresh Tomatoes and Olives

Boiled Beef and Vegetables with Green Sauce

Veal Pizzaiola

Osso Buco

Veal Milanese

CHICKEN MARSALA

Add a light pasta or risotto and Sauteed Peas with Prosciutto (page 134) and you're all set for company.

Makes 4 servings

3 tablespoons all-purpose flour
$^1/_4$ teaspoon salt
Freshly ground black pepper, to taste
1 tablespoon + 1 teaspoon reduced-calorie tub margarine
2 teaspoons olive oil
Four 3-ounce skinless boneless chicken breasts, pounded $^1/_4$" thick

2 cups thinly sliced white mushrooms
8 fluid ounces (1 cup) dry Marsala wine
2 tablespoons minced fresh flat-leaf parsley
1 tablespoon minced fresh basil (or $^1/_2$ teaspoon dried)
1 clove garlic, bruised

1. On a large sheet of wax paper, combine the flour, salt and pepper.
2. Place a large nonstick skillet over medium heat 30 seconds; heat the margarine and oil 30 seconds more.
3. Being sure to coat both sides evenly, quickly dip the chicken in the flour mixture; shake off any excess. Place in the skillet and cook, 5 minutes, turning once, until golden brown. Transfer to a warm platter.
4. In the same skillet, combine the mushrooms, wine, parsley, basil and garlic; cook, stirring frequently and scraping up any browned bits from the bottom of the pan, 5 minutes, until the liquid is reduced to about $^1/_3$ cup. Remove and discard the garlic.
5. Reduce the heat to low. Return the chicken and any accumulated juices to the skillet; cook 1 minute, until heated through. Place one chicken breast and an equal amount of sauce on each of 4 plates and serve.

Serving (2 ounces chicken with 1 tablespoon sauce) provides: 1 Fat, 1 Vegetable, 2 Proteins, $^1/_4$ Bread, 50 Optional Calories.

Per Serving: 261 Calories, 6 g Total Fat, 1 g Saturated Fat, 49 mg Cholesterol, 226 mg Sodium, 14 g Total Carbohydrate, 1 g Dietary Fiber, 21 g Protein, 25 mg Calcium.

ROASTED CHICKEN WITH POTATOES AND ONIONS

This one-pot meal takes just minutes to prepare and about an hour to bake. Fix is for Sunday supper and brown bag any leftovers during the week.

Makes 8 servings

1 cup low-sodium chicken broth
$^1/_2$ cup fresh lemon juice
$^1/_4$ cup minced fresh thyme leaves (or 2 teaspoons dried leaves, crumbled)
2 tablespoons + 2 teaspoons olive oil
$^1/_4$ teaspoon salt

Freshly ground black pepper, to taste
2 pounds 8 ounces pared all-purpose potatoes, cubed
4 medium onions, coarsely chopped
Eight 3-ounce skinless boneless chicken breasts

1. Preheat the oven to 350° F. Spray a 13 × 9" baking dish with nonstick cooking spray.
2. In a large bowl, combine the broth, juice, thyme, oil, salt and pepper. Add the potatoes and onions; toss to coat. With a slotted spoon, transfer the solids to the prepared baking dish. Add the chicken to the broth mixture; toss to coat. Transfer the chicken to the baking dish, arranging the chicken and vegetables in a single layer; pour the broth mixture evenly over all. Cover with foil.
3. Roast 30 minutes, turning the chicken occasionally, until the juices run pink when the chicken is pierced with a fork. Remove the foil and roast 30 minutes more, until the vegetables are golden and the juices run clear when the chicken is pierced with a fork. Divide evenly among 8 plates and serve.

Serving (2 ounces chicken with 4 ounces potatoes and $^1/_4$ cup onion) provides: 1 Fat, $^1/_2$ Vegetable, 2 Proteins, 1 Bread, 5 Optional Calories.

Per Serving: 270 Calories, 6 g Total Fat, 1 g Saturated Fat, 49 mg Cholesterol, 147 mg Sodium, 31 g Total Carbohydrate, 3 g Dietary Fiber, 24 g Protein, 38 mg Calcium.

BEEF-STUFFED FRYING PEPPERS

Stuffed peppers are freezer and lunchbox friendly. Delicious hot or cold and colorful as well, they're also perfect for a buffet supper or picnic.

Makes 4 servings

10 ounces lean ground beef
(10% or less fat)
1 medium tomato, finely chopped
2 medium onions, finely chopped
1 medium yellow or red bell
pepper, finely chopped
3 egg whites
3 tablespoons plain dried bread
crumbs

1 tablespoon minced fresh oregano
(or 1 teaspoon dried)
$1/4$ teaspoon salt
Freshly ground black pepper,
to taste
4 large Italian frying peppers,
halved lengthwise, and seeded
1 cup tomato sauce (no salt added)

1. Preheat the oven to 400° F. Spray a 13 × 9" baking dish with nonstick cooking spray.
2. In a medium bowl, combine the beef, tomato, onions, bell pepper, egg whites, bread crumbs, oregano, salt and black pepper; set aside.
3. Place the frying peppers in a microwavable baking dish. With a vented cover, microwave on medium 6 minutes, until tender. Uncover and let cool. Fill the pepper halves evenly with the beef mixture, pressing in the mixture lightly with a fork. Place in the prepared baking dish and bake 25–30 minutes, until the filling is slightly browned. Spoon 2 tablespoons of the tomato sauce over each pepper half and bake 15–20 minutes more, until the sauce is bubbling and slightly browned. Place 2 stuffed pepper halves on each of 4 plates and serve hot or cold.

Serving (2 stuffed pepper halves) provides: $5^{1}/_{2}$ Vegetables, $2^{1}/_{4}$ Proteins, $1/4$ Bread.

Per Serving: 240 Calories, 8 g Total Fat, 3 g Saturated Fat, 44 mg Cholesterol, 294 mg Sodium, 23 g Total Carbohydrate, 4 g Dietary Fiber, 21 g Protein, 47 mg Calcium.

GRILLED SIRLOIN WITH FRESH TOMATOES AND OLIVES

Topping grilled or broiled steak with two quintessentially Mediterranean foods gives it a whole new flavor.

Makes 4 servings

4 large or 8 small fresh plum tomatoes, peeled, seeded and chopped*

12 large or 20 small imported black olives, pitted and sliced

1 tablespoon minced fresh oregano (or $^1/_2$ teaspoon dried)

2 garlic cloves, minced

Freshly ground black pepper, to taste

15 ounces lean well-trimmed boneless sirloin steak

1. Spray the broiler or grill rack with nonstick cooking spray; place 5" from heat. Preheat the broiler or prepare the grill according to the manufacturer's instructions.
2. Spray a medium nonstick skillet with nonstick cooking spray; place over medium heat 30 seconds. Add the tomatoes, olives, oregano, garlic and pepper; cook, stirring frequently, 5 minutes, until thickened. Set aside and keep warm.
3. Broil or grill the steak on the prepared rack 10 minutes (rare), 12 minutes (medium) or 14 minutes (well-done), turning once. Transfer to a cutting board and let stand 5 minutes before slicing. Divide evenly among 4 plates, top each portion with $^1/_4$ cup of the sauce and serve at once.

Serving (3 ounces steak with $^1/_4$ cup sauce) provides: $^1/_2$ Fat, 1 Vegetable, 3 Proteins.

Per Serving: 198 Calories, 8 g Total Fat, 3 g Saturated Fat, 76 mg Cholesterol, 185 mg Sodium, 4 g Total Carbohydrate, 1 g Dietary Fiber, 26 g Protein, 30 mg Calcium.

*If fresh plum tomatoes are not available, substitute an equal number of chopped drained canned Italian plum tomatoes (no salt added).

BOILED BEEF AND VEGETABLES WITH GREEN SAUCE

This simplified version of a little-known Italian dish just keeps giving and giving: the meat and some of the vegetables make two hearty meals for four; the broth and the remaining vegetables with potatoes, pasta or rice make a great soup; and there's still plenty of broth left over to freeze for other uses.

Makes 8 servings

$^1/_2$ cup chopped fresh flat-leaf
   parsley
1 tablespoon chopped fresh mint
   leaves
1 tablespoon rinsed drained capers
1 tablespoon prepared white
   horseradish
2 teaspoons olive oil
1 teaspoon white wine vinegar
1 rinsed drained anchovy fillet
   (or $^1/_2$ teaspoon anchovy paste)
4 medium onions, chopped

8 medium celery stalks, chopped
2 medium carrots, diced
1 small head green cabbage, cored
   and cut into 8 equal pieces
2 pounds lean beef (brisket, rump,
   bottom round or lean chuck)
2 cups chopped canned plum
   tomatoes (no salt added), with
   juice
$^1/_4$ teaspoon salt
Freshly ground black pepper,
   to taste

1. To prepare the sauce, in a mini food processor or blender, combine the parsley, mint, capers, horseradish, oil, vinegar and anchovy; purée until smooth.
2. Place the onions, celery, carrots and cabbage in a large saucepan or Dutch oven; add cold water to cover. Bring to a boil. Add the beef, cover the saucepan and bring back to a boil. Reduce the heat to low; simmer about 15 minutes, skimming off any foam that accumulates on the surface. Stir in the tomatoes, salt and pepper; simmer about 2 hours more, until the meat and vegetables are very tender. Transfer the meat and vegetables to a platter, reserving the broth (and some vegetables, if desired) for later use.
3. Divide the beef and vegetables evenly among 8 plates and serve with 1 tablespoon green sauce on the side.

Serving (3 ounces beef with 2 cups vegetables and 1 tablespoon sauce) provides: $^1/_4$ Fat, $3^1/_2$ Vegetables, 3 Proteins.

Per Serving: 246 Calories, 10 g Total Fat, 3 g Saturated Fat, 71 mg Cholesterol, 260 mg Sodium, 13 g Total Carbohydrate, 4 g Dietary Fiber, 26 g Protein, 83 mg Calcium.

VEAL PIZZAIOLA

Some Italian cooks dip the meat in bread crumbs before sauteing it; others insist on adding capers to the sauce. But most believe that "less is more," and that it's the fresh oregano that really gives this dish its distinctive flavor. Pasta-Stuffed Peppers (page 139), Risotto with Swiss Chard and Tomatoes (page 83) or Rotelle with Greens (page 51) would be great with the veal.

Makes 4 servings

1 tablespoon + 1 teaspoon olive oil

15 ounces veal cutlets, pounded
¹/₄" thick

2 cups chopped drained canned
plum tomatoes (no salt added)

4 fluid ounces (¹/₂ cup) dry white
wine

2 tablespoons minced fresh oregano

2 garlic cloves, minced

¹/₄ teaspoon salt

Freshly ground black pepper,
to taste

1. Place a large nonstick skillet over medium heat 30 seconds; heat the oil 30 seconds more. Add the veal; cook, turning once, 3–5 minutes, until browned on both sides. Transfer to a warm platter.
2. In the same skillet, combine the tomatoes, wine, oregano, garlic, salt and pepper. Reduce the heat to medium-low and cook 5 minutes, until the tomatoes are slightly softened.
3. Return the veal and any accumulated juices to the skillet and spoon the tomato mixture over it. Reduce the heat to low; simmer 15–20 minutes, until the sauce is thickened and the veal is cooked through and very tender. Divide evenly among 4 plates and serve.

Serving (3 ounces veal with ¹/₄ cup sauce) provides: 1 Fat, 1 Vegetable, 3 Proteins, 25 Optional Calories.

Per Serving: 201 Calories, 7 g Total Fat, 1 g Saturated Fat, 83 mg Cholesterol, 221 mg Sodium, 6 g Total Carbohydrate, 1 g Dietary Fiber, 24 g Protein, 52 mg Calcium.

OSSO BUCO

Ask your butcher for meat from the center part of the shank, where the bone is smaller. Start the meal with a vegetable antipasto, then serve this classic and classy Milanese dish with—what else—Risotto Milanese (page 86).

Makes 4 servings

$^1/_3$ cup + 2 teaspoons all-purpose flour

Four 8-ounce well-trimmed veal shanks,* cut about 1" thick

2 tablespoons + 2 teaspoons reduced-calorie tub margarine

$1^1/_2$ cups sliced white or wild mushrooms

6 medium shallots, finely chopped

$^1/_2$ medium carrot, finely chopped

2 medium celery stalks, finely chopped

4 fluid ounces ($^1/_2$ cup) dry white wine

1 garlic clove, minced

1 cup low-sodium beef broth

2 tablespoons minced fresh flat-leaf parsley

1 tablespoon freshly grated lemon zest†

2 tablespoons fresh lemon juice

1 tablespoon minced fresh rosemary leaves (or $^1/_2$ teaspoon dried leaves, crumbled)

1 tablespoon minced fresh sage leaves (or $^1/_2$ teaspoon dried leaves, crumbled)

1 rinsed drained anchovy fillet, chopped (or $^1/_2$ teaspoon anchovy paste)

Freshly ground black pepper, to taste

1. Place the flour in a shallow bowl. Dredge the veal in the flour; set aside.
2. Place a large nonstick saucepan or Dutch oven over medium heat 30 seconds; melt the margarine 30 seconds more. Add the veal; cook, turning once, 10 minutes, until browned. Set aside.
3. In the same saucepan, combine the mushrooms, shallots, carrot, celery, wine and garlic; cook, stirring constantly and scraping up any browned bits from the bottom of the pan, 2 minutes, until the liquid is reduced to about $^1/_4$ cup. Add the broth, parsley, zest, juice, rosemary, sage, anchovy and pepper. Return the veal to the saucepan. Cover and reduce the heat to low; simmer, adding $^1/_4$ cup water at a time as needed, $1–1^1/_2$ hours, until the veal is very tender. Place one veal shank on each of 4 plates; spoon one-fourth of the sauce over each portion and serve.

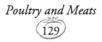
Serving (1 veal shank with ¹/₄ cup sauce) provides: 1 Fat, 1¹/₂ Vegetables, 3 Proteins, ¹/₂ Bread, 30 Optional Calories.

Per Serving: 273 Calories, 8 g Total Fat, 2 g Saturated Fat, 89 mg Total Cholesterol, 207 mg Sodium, 17 g Total Carbohydrate, 2 g Dietary Fiber, 28 g Protein, 40 mg Calcium.

One 8-ounce veal shank will yield a 3 ounce cooked trimmed edible portion.

†The zest of the lemon is the peel without any of the pith (white membrane). To remove zest from lemon, use a zester or the fine side of a vegetable grater.

VEAL MILANESE

Just a little lemon goes a long way toward enhancing the flavor of this northern Italian dish. Accompanied by Arugula and Potato Salad (page 105), it becomes an exquisite luncheon or light dinner.

Makes 4 servings

3 egg whites
$^1/_3$ cup + 2 teaspoons plain dried bread crumbs
$^1/_4$ teaspoon salt
Freshly ground black pepper, to taste
2 tablespoons + 2 teaspoons reduced-calorie tub margarine

Four 3-ounce veal cutlets, pounded $^1/_4$" thick
1 lemon, quartered
2 tablespoons minced fresh flat-leaf parsley

1. In a small bowl, beat the egg whites 10–15 seconds, until foamy; transfer to a shallow bowl.
2. On a large sheet of wax paper, combine the bread crumbs, salt and pepper.
3. Place a large nonstick skillet over medium-high heat 30 seconds; melt the margarine 30 seconds more.
4. Coating both sides evenly, quickly dip the cutlets, one at a time, into the egg whites, then the bread crumbs. Place in the hot skillet; cook, turning once, 3–5 minutes, until golden brown. Place one cutlet on each of 4 warm plates. Squeeze 1 lemon wedge over each, sprinkle evenly with parsley and serve.

Serving (2 ounces veal) provides: 1 Fat, $2^1/_4$ Proteins, $^1/_2$ Bread.

Per Serving: 196 Calories, 7 g Total Fat, 2 g Saturated Fat, 66 mg Cholesterol, 376 mg Sodium, 11 g Total Carbohydrate, 1 g Dietary Fiber, 22 g Protein, 49 mg Calcium.

10

VEGETABLES

Sauteed Broccoli with Garlic and Lemon

Sauteed Mushrooms with Mint and Parsley

Sauteed Peas with Prosciutto

Sauteed Peppers

Sweet and Sour Onions

Broccoli Rabe with Potatoes

Cannellini-Stuffed Peppers

Pasta-Stuffed Peppers

Roasted Potatoes with Oregano

Rosemary-Roasted Potatoes, Onions and Carrots

Potatoes and Green Beans with Basil Pesto

Roasted Radicchio and Endive with Mozzarella

Ciambotta

Stewed Artichokes

Baked Eggplant Parmigiana

Eggplant Torta

Sauteed Broccoli with Garlic and Lemon

Garlic and lemon are the classic dressing for many an Italian vegetable dish or salad. This dressing is good with cauliflower, broccoli rabe or greens such as Swiss chard or spinach, and it's a never-fail pasta topper.

Makes 4 servings

4 cups bite-size broccoli florets	6 medium garlic cloves, minced
1/2 cup low-sodium chicken broth	1/4 teaspoon salt
1 tablespoon + 1 teaspoon olive oil	2 tablespoons fresh lemon juice

1. In a large saucepan, bring 2" water to a boil. Arrange the broccoli on a steamer rack; place in the saucepan and cover with a tight-fitting lid. Steam 3 minutes, until barely tender.
2. In a large nonstick skillet, combine the broth and oil over medium-high heat. Add the broccoli, garlic and salt. Cook, stirring frequently, about 5 minutes, until the broccoli is tender and the liquid is evaporated.
3. Transfer to a serving bowl; sprinkle with the juice. Let stand until slightly warm or at room temperature. Divide evenly among 4 plates and serve.

Serving (1 cup) provides: 1 Fat, 2 Vegetables, 5 Optional Calories.

Per Serving: 71 Calories, 5 g Total Fat, 1 g Saturated Fat, 0 mg Cholesterol, 169 mg Sodium, 6 g Total Carbohydrate, 2 g Dietary Fiber, 3 g Protein, 45 mg Calcium.

SAUTEED MUSHROOMS WITH MINT AND PARSLEY

The trick here is to slice the mushrooms thinly. In Italy, mint, or even catmint (we know it as catnip), is sometimes used with mushrooms.

Makes 4 servings

2 teaspoons olive oil
3 medium shallots, finely chopped
2 medium garlic cloves, minced
3 cups white mushrooms, trimmed and sliced very thin
1¹/₂ cups portobello mushrooms, trimmed and sliced very thin

¹/₄ teaspoon salt
¹/₄ teaspoon ground white pepper
2 tablespoons minced fresh mint leaves
2 tablespoons minced fresh flat-leaf parsley

1. Place a large nonstick skillet over medium heat 30 seconds; heat the oil 30 seconds more. Add the shallots and garlic; cook, stirring constantly, 1 minute, until the garlic and shallots become fragrant.

2. Add the mushrooms, salt and pepper. Cook over medium heat, stirring frequently, 5–6 minutes, until the mushrooms have released some of their liquid.

3. Add the mint and parsley. Raise the heat to high; cook, stirring constantly, 3 minutes, until the liquid is evaporated. Divide evenly among 4 plates and serve warm or at room temperature.

Serving (¹/₂ cup) provides: ¹/₂ Fat, 2¹/₄ Vegetables.

Per Serving: 56 Calories, 3 g Total Fat, 0 g Saturated Fat, 0 mg Cholesterol, 141 mg Sodium, 7 g Total Carbohydrate, 1 g Dietary Fiber, 2 g Protein, 16 mg Calcium.

Sauteed Peas with Prosciutto

In Florence, they use the tiniest fresh peas imaginable in this dish. If you don't have the time to shell fresh peas, use frozen, but be sure they're the really small ones.

Makes 4 servings

1 tablespoon + 1 teaspoon olive oil
2 medium shallots, minced
2 medium garlic cloves, minced
1 ounce well-trimmed prosciutto, minced
2 cups fresh or partially thawed frozen young green peas

1 tablespoon minced fresh mint leaves
$1/4$ teaspoon salt
Freshly ground black pepper, to taste

1. Place a large nonstick skillet over medium heat 30 seconds; heat the oil 30 seconds more. Add the shallots, garlic and prosciutto; cook, stirring constantly, 1 minute, until shallots are wilted.
2. Add the peas, mint, salt, pepper and 3 tablespoons water. Cover and cook 3–5 minutes if using frozen peas or 10 minutes if using fresh peas, until the peas are tender but not mushy. Divide evenly among 4 plates and serve at once.

Serving ($1/2$ cup) provides: 1 Fat, $1/4$ Protein, 1 Bread.

Per Serving: 122 Calories, 6 g Total Fat, 1 g Saturated Fat, 6 mg Cholesterol, 271 mg Sodium, 12 g Total Carbohydrate, 3 g Dietary Fiber, 6 g Protein, 25 mg Calcium.

SAUTEED PEPPERS

When you taste the soft, creamy texture and the concentrated flavor of these peppers, you'll swear there has to be more than just half a teaspoon of oil per serving. Serve them as an appetizer or a side dish, layer them on your favorite sandwich, or toss them into a salad.

Makes 4 servings

4 medium green and red Italian frying peppers, quartered and seeded	$^1/_4$ teaspoon salt
	Freshly ground black pepper, to taste
4 medium garlic cloves, sliced	1 teaspoon balsamic vinegar
2 teaspoons olive oil	

1. In a large nonstick skillet over medium-low heat, combine the frying peppers, 1 cup hot water, the garlic, oil, salt and black pepper. Cover; cook, stirring occasionally and adding $^1/_2$ cup water as needed, 20 minutes, until the peppers are tender and the liquid is evaporated.
2. Add the balsamic vinegar; toss lightly. Divide evenly among 4 plates and serve hot, warm or at room temperature.

Serving (1 cup) provides: $^1/_2$ Fat, 2 Vegetables.

Per Serving: 58 Calories, 2 g Total Fat, 0 g Saturated Fat, 0 mg Cholesterol, 141 mg Sodium, 9 g Total Carbohydrate, 1 g Dietary Fiber, 2 g Protein, 21 mg Calcium.

SWEET AND SOUR ONIONS

Pearl onions, simmered in vinegar and a bit of sugar, make a delectable accompaniment to meat or fowl, a great antipasto component, garnish or snack. Don't even think of peeling so many fresh onions; use frozen ones.

Makes 4 servings

4 cups thawed frozen pearl onions
2 cups low-sodium beef broth
2 tablespoons + 2 teaspoons
reduced-calorie tub margarine

2 tablespoons white wine vinegar
1 tablespoon granulated sugar
Freshly ground black pepper,
to taste

1. In a large nonstick skillet over medium-low heat, combine the onions, broth and margarine. Cover; cook, stirring occasionally and adding 1 tablespoon water at a time as needed, 30 minutes, until the onions begin to soften.
2. Add the vinegar, sugar and pepper; cook, stirring frequently and adding 1 tablespoon water at a time, as needed, 30 minutes more, or until the onions are very tender. Divide evenly among 4 plates and serve.

Serving (1 cup) provides: 1 Fat, 2 Vegetables, 20 Optional Calories.

Per Serving: 137 Calories, 5 g Total Fat, 1 g Saturated Fat, 0 mg Cholesterol, 110 mg Sodium, 19 g Total Carbohydrate, 0 g Dietary Fiber, 4 g Protein, 68 mg Calcium.

BROCCOLI RABE WITH POTATOES

Broccoli rabe has a pleasantly bitter flavor that stands up well to crushed red pepper and a hefty amount of garlic. Adding crisp potato slices makes it even more special, and a great accompaniment to meat or fowl.

Makes 4 servings

6 cups coarsely chopped well-washed trimmed broccoli rabe

1 tablespoon + 1 teaspoon olive oil

1 pound 4 ounces pared all-purpose potatoes, cut into $1/8$" slices

4 garlic cloves, minced

$1/2$ teaspoon crushed red pepper flakes

$1/4$ teaspoon salt

1. In a large saucepan, bring 2" water to a boil. Arrange the broccoli rabe on a steamer rack; place in the saucepan and cover with a tight-fitting lid. Steam 10 minutes, until tender.

2. In a large nonstick skillet over medium-low heat, heat the oil and spread it to cover bottom of pan. Arrange the potatoes evenly in the pan, overlapping if necessary. Sprinkle with the garlic, pepper flakes and salt. Cook until potatoes are browned on the bottom but are still not quite tender.

3. Spread the broccoli rabe evenly over the potatoes. Cover and cook, adding $1/4$ cup water at a time as needed, 10-15 minutes, until the potatoes are tender. Divide evenly among 4 plates and serve hot or at room temperature.

Serving (2 cups) provides: 1 Fat, 3 Vegetables, 1 Bread.

Per Serving: 185 Calories, 5 g Total Fat, 1 g Saturated Fat, 0 mg Cholesterol, 195 mg Sodium, 32 g Total Carbohydrate, 5 g Dietary Fiber, 6 g Protein, 90 mg Calcium.

CANNELLINI-STUFFED PEPPERS

In Tuscany, beans—especially the white kidney beans called cannellini—are the staff of life. Here, combined with sage and tomatoes, they provide a hearty filling for colorful bell peppers. You'll want to include these flavorsome, healthful gems in your menu plans all year round.

Makes 4 servings

4 medium red or yellow bell peppers, halved lengthwise, seeded and deveined
1 tablespoon + 1 teaspoon olive oil
8 large plum tomatoes, peeled, seeded and chopped
2 medium onions, minced
2 tablespoons minced fresh sage (or 1 teaspoon dried)

1 garlic clove, minced
$^1/_4$ teaspoon salt
Freshly ground black pepper, to taste
1 pound drained cooked cannellini (white kidney) beans

1. Preheat the oven to 425° F. Rinse the peppers under cold running water. Place in a 13 × 9" baking dish; cover with foil and bake 20 minutes, until tender-crisp. Uncover and bake 15 minutes more. Remove from the oven; drain, cover and set aside.
2. Place a medium nonstick skillet over medium-high heat 30 seconds; heat the oil 30 seconds more. Add the tomatoes, onions, sage, garlic, salt and black pepper; cook, stirring frequently, 5 minutes, until the sauce is thickened and the onions are softened. Remove from the heat; stir in the beans.
3. Divide the bean mixture evenly among the pepper halves. Place 2 pepper halves on each of 4 plates and serve.

Serving (2 stuffed pepper halves) provides: 1 Fat, $4^1/_2$ Vegetables, 2 Proteins.

Per Serving: 248 Calories, 6 g Total Fat, 1 g Saturated Fat, 0 mg Cholesterol, 150 mg Sodium, 41 g Total Carbohydrate, 8 g Dietary Fiber, 12 g Protein, 59 mg Calcium.

PASTA-STUFFED PEPPERS

Baked peppers, filled with small pasta and accented with capers, anchovies, mushrooms, tomatoes and mozzarella cheese, are a novel and satisfying entrée.

Makes 4 servings

1 tablespoon + 1 teaspoon olive oil
1 medium onion, minced
2 garlic cloves, minced
4 large or 8 small plum tomatoes, peeled, seeded and chopped
1 cup chopped white mushrooms
1 tablespoon minced fresh basil (or 1 teaspoon dried)
1 tablespoon minced fresh oregano or marjoram (or 1 teaspoon dried)
1 tablespoon rinsed drained capers, chopped

2 rinsed drained anchovy fillets, chopped (or 1 teaspoon anchovy paste)
Freshly ground black pepper, to taste
3 ounces small star, orzo or other small pasta
3 ounces skim-milk mozzarella cheese, shredded
4 medium green, red or yellow bell peppers, halved lengthwise, and seeded

1. Preheat the oven to 350° F. Spray a 13 × 9" baking dish with nonstick cooking spray.
2. Place a medium nonstick skillet over medium heat 30 seconds; heat the oil 30 seconds more. Add the onion and garlic; cook, stirring frequently, 3–4 minutes, until the onion is pale gold. Stir in the tomatoes, mushrooms, basil, oregano, capers, anchovies and black pepper. Cook about 5 minutes more, until thickened. Remove from the heat and set aside.
3. In a pot of boiling water, cook the pasta 5 minutes, until barely tender. Drain and transfer to a bowl; toss with half the cheese and all the sauce.
4. Divide the pasta mixture evenly among the pepper halves. Place the pepper halves in the prepared baking dish. Pour $1/2$" water in the bottom of the dish. Bake 45 minutes, until the peppers are tender. Sprinkle the remaining cheese over the filling; bake about 5 minutes more, until the cheese is melted. Place 2 pepper halves on each of 4 plates and serve hot or warm.

Serving (2 stuffed pepper halves) provides: 1 Fat, $3^3/_4$ Vegetables, 1 Protein, 1 Bread, 5 Optional Calories.

Per Serving: 206 Calories, 6 g Total Fat, 1 g Saturated Fat, 3 mg Cholesterol, 296 mg Sodium, 28 g Total Carbohydrate, 3 g Dietary Fiber, 12 g Protein, 188 mg Calcium.

ROASTED POTATOES WITH OREGANO

Crisp on the outside and tender on the inside, roasted potatoes are always wonderful. With oregano, they're especially fragrant and delicious—and they couldn't be easier to prepare.

Makes 4 servings

2 tablespoons minced fresh oregano
   (or 1 teaspoon dried)
2 teaspoons olive oil
¼ teaspoon salt

Freshly ground black pepper,
   to taste
1 pound 4 ounces pared all-purpose
   potatoes, cut into 1½" chunks

1. Preheat the oven to 400° F.
2. In an 8" square baking pan, combine the oregano, oil, salt and pepper. Add the potatoes; toss to coat.
3. Roast, turning the potatoes once, about 45 minutes, until the potatoes are golden and crisp on the outside and tender on the inside. Divide evenly among 4 plates and serve at once.

Serving (4 ounces) provides: ½ Fat, 1 Bread.

Per Serving: 133 Calories, 2 g Total Fat, 0 g Saturated Fat, 0 mg Cholesterol, 144 mg Sodium, 26 g Total Carbohydrate, 2 g Dietary Fiber, 3 g Protein, 17 mg Calcium.

ROSEMARY-ROASTED POTATOES, ONIONS AND CARROTS

Italian cooks are experts at waking up the flavors of ordinary dishes with herbs. With a generous sprinkling of rosemary and sage, that's just what happens to these three vegetables.

Makes 4 servings

2 tablespoons low-sodium chicken or vegetable broth
1 tablespoon + 1 teaspoon olive oil
1 tablespoon minced fresh rosemary leaves (or $^1/_2$ teaspoon dried)
1 tablespoon minced fresh sage leaves (or $^1/_2$ teaspoon dried)

$^1/_4$ teaspoon salt
Freshly ground black pepper, to taste
1 pound 4 ounces potatoes, scrubbed and cut into $^1/_4$" slices
2 medium onions, sliced
1 medium carrot, diced

1. Preheat the oven to 425° F. Spray a 13 × 9" baking dish with nonstick cooking spray.
2. In a large bowl, combine the broth, oil, rosemary, sage, salt and pepper. Add the potatoes, onions and carrot; toss to coat.
3. Spread the vegetable mixture evenly in the prepared baking dish; cover with foil. Roast 30 minutes, until barely tender; remove the foil and roast 30 minutes more, until crisp and golden. Divide evenly among 4 plates and serve.

Serving (1 cup) provides: 1 Fat, 1 Vegetable, 1 Bread.

Per Serving: 182 Calories, 5 g Total Fat, 1 g Saturated Fat, 0 mg Cholesterol, 157 mg Sodium, 32 g Total Carbohydrate, 4 g Dietary Fiber, 4 g Protein, 30 mg Calcium.

POTATOES AND GREEN BEANS WITH BASIL PESTO

Basil pesto really perks up these two common vegetables. Let this recipe inspire you to use pesto on other vegetable combinations.

Makes 4 servings

2 cups packed fresh basil leaves
1 tablespoon + 1 teaspoon olive oil
2 garlic cloves, minced
$^1/_4$ teaspoon salt
Freshly ground black pepper,
   to taste

1 pound 4 ounces pared all-purpose
   potatoes, cut into $1^1/_2$" chunks
4 cups sliced green beans

1. In a food processor, combine the basil, oil, garlic, salt and pepper; pulse several times until smooth. Set aside.
2. Place the potatoes in a medium saucepan; add cold water to cover. Cover and bring water to a boil; reduce the heat to low and simmer 20 minutes, until tender. Drain and place in a large serving bowl.
3. Meanwhile, in a large saucepan, bring 2" water to a boil. Arrange the green beans on a steamer rack; place in the saucepan and cover with a tight-fitting lid. Steam 5–6 minutes, until tender-crisp. Transfer to the bowl with the potatoes.
4. Add the pesto; toss to coat well. Divide evenly among 4 plates and serve warm or at room temperature.

Serving ($^3/_4$ cup) provides: 1 Fat, 2 Vegetables, 1 Bread.

Per Serving: 222 Calories, 5 g Total Fat, 1 g Saturated Fat, 0 mg Cholesterol, 155 mg Sodium, 42 g Total Carbohydrate, 4 g Dietary Fiber, 7 g Protein, 339 mg Calcium.

ROASTED RADICCHIO AND ENDIVE WITH MOZZARELLA

The Italians roast, bake and grill vegetables that most Americans haven't let out of their salad bowls. If you've never tried either of these vegetables cooked, this recipe is a perfect introduction.

Makes 4 servings

1 medium head radicchio, washed, trimmed and cut into 4 wedges
2 medium heads Belgian endive, washed, trimmed and halved lengthwise

2 teaspoons olive oil
3 ounces skim-milk mozzarella cheese, shredded

1. Preheat the oven to 400° F. Spray a 13 × 9" baking dish with nonstick cooking spray.
2. Place the radicchio and endive, cut-sides up, in the prepared dish. Drizzle evenly with the oil.
3. Roast 10–15 minutes, until tender. Sprinkle evenly with the mozzarella; bake about 5 minutes more, until the cheese is melted. Divide evenly among 4 plates and serve hot.

Serving (¹/₄ radicchio and ¹/₂ endive, with ³/₄ ounce cheese) provides:
¹/₂ Fat, 1¹/₂ Vegetables, 1 Protein.

Per Serving: 70 Calories, 3 g Total Fat, 0 g Saturated Fat, 2 mg Cholesterol, 165 mg Sodium, 5 g Total Carbohydrate, 2 g Dietary Fiber, 8 g Protein, 172 mg Calcium.

CIAMBOTTA

MIXED VEGETABLE STEW

This Italian version of ratatouille uses four different colors of bell peppers. If your market doesn't have all of them, feel free to mix or match whatever is available. The stew can be partially prepared a few hours ahead of time.

Makes 4 servings

$^1/_2$ cup low-sodium vegetable broth
1 tablespoon olive oil
$^1/_4$ teaspoon salt
Freshly ground black pepper, to taste
1 medium eggplant, cut crosswise into $^1/_4$" slices
1 pound 4 ounces potatoes, scrubbed and cut into $^1/_8$" slices
1 medium green bell pepper, seeded and cut crosswise into $^1/_4$" slices
1 medium yellow bell pepper, seeded and cut crosswise into $^1/_4$" slices

1 medium red bell pepper, seeded and cut crosswise into $^1/_4$" slices
1 medium orange bell pepper, seeded and cut crosswise into $^1/_4$" slices
1 medium zucchini, cut crosswise into $^1/_4$" slices
3 medium tomatoes, peeled, seeded and chopped
3 garlic cloves, minced

1. Spray the broiler or grill rack with nonstick cooking spray; place 5" from heat. Preheat the broiler, or prepare the grill according to the manufacturer's instructions.
2. In a small bowl, whisk together the broth, oil, salt and pepper. With a pastry brush, lightly coat the eggplant, potatoes, peppers and zucchini on both sides with the broth mixture.
3. Broil or grill the eggplant, potatoes, peppers and zucchini 5 minutes, until tender and slightly charred; turn and broil or grill 4 minutes more. Remove from the heat.
4. Preheat oven to 375° F, unless planning to bake at another time. Spray a 4-quart casserole with nonstick cooking spray. Place the eggplant in the bottom of the casserole; sprinkle evenly with one-fourth of the tomatoes and garlic. Add the potatoes and another fourth of the tomatoes and garlic. Repeat with the peppers and end with the zucchini, sprinkling each layer with another fourth of the tomatoes and garlic. (The dish can be prepared up to 2 hours ahead at this point; cover and keep at room temperature.)

5. Bake, uncovered, 30–40 minutes, until bubbling. Divide evenly among 4 plates and serve hot, warm or at room temperature.

Serving (1 cup) provides: $^3/_4$ Fats, $5^1/_2$ Vegetables, 1 Bread, 5 Optional Calories.

Per Serving: 270 Calories, 8 g Total Fat, 1 g Saturated Fat, 0 mg Cholesterol, 172 mg Sodium, 48 g Total Carbohydrate, 7 g Dietary Fiber, 7 g Protein, 81 mg Calcium.

STEWED ARTICHOKES

If you like artichokes, you'll love them stewed in white wine, garlic, lemon and oil until they're meltingly tender. Rich in fiber and flavor, they're great paired with almost any pasta, or try them with your favorite meat, fish or poultry.

Makes 4 servings

$^1/_4$ cup fresh lemon juice
4 medium artichokes
1 tablespoon + 1 teaspoon extra virgin olive oil
6 medium shallots, chopped
8 fluid ounces (1 cup) dry white wine

2 tablespoons minced fresh flat-leaf parsley
2 garlic cloves, minced
$^1/_4$ teaspoon salt
Freshly ground black pepper, to taste

1. Fill a large bowl three-fourths full with cold water; stir in the juice.
2. Slice off the stem and upper third of the artichokes so they have flat bottoms and tops. Trim the tough outer leaves and remove the chokes with a teaspoon. Cut in half lengthwise; drop into the water-juice mixture to prevent discoloration.
3. Place a medium saucepan over medium heat 30 seconds; heat the oil 30 seconds more. Add the shallots; cook 1 minute, until wilted. Drain the artichokes; add to the saucepan with the wine, parsley, garlic, salt and pepper. Cover; reduce the heat to medium-low. Cook 40 minutes, adding 1 tablespoon water at a time as needed, until the artichoke hearts are tender. Divide evenly among 4 plates and serve warm or at room temperature.

Serving (2 artichoke halves) provides: 1 Fat, $1^1/_4$ Vegetables, 50 Optional Calories.

Per Serving: 166 Calories, 5 g Total Fat, 1 g Saturated Fat, 0 mg Cholesterol, 270 mg Sodium, 20 g Total Carbohydrate, 7 g Dietary Fiber, 5 g Protein, 80 mg Calcium.

BAKED EGGPLANT PARMIGIANA

Eggplant is at its best when it's baked and combined with tomatoes, herbs and delicious melted mozzarella. Make a double batch: reheated and piled on crusty Italian bread, this makes a fantastic sandwich.

Makes 4 servings

1 medium eggplant, pared and cut into $^1/_4$" slices

1$^1/_2$ cups Tomato-Herb Sauce (page 21)

$^1/_3$ cup + 2 teaspoons plain dried bread crumbs

3 ounces skim-milk mozzarella cheese, shredded

1. Preheat the oven to 350° F. Spray 2 baking sheets with nonstick cooking spray. Spray an 8" square baking dish with nonstick cooking spray.
2. Arrange the eggplant slices in a single layer on the baking sheets. Bake 15–20 minutes, until tender.
3. Spread one-fourth of the sauce on the bottom of the baking dish. Arrange the eggplant slices in a single layer, slightly overlapping if necessary. Sprinkle with one-third of the bread crumbs and cheese and another fourth of the sauce. Repeat the layers, finishing with a layer of eggplant topped with the last fourth of the sauce. Cover with foil and bake 30–40 minutes, until heated through and bubbling. Remove the foil; increase the heat to 400° F and bake 15 minutes more, until the top is slightly crisp. Divide evenly among 4 plates and serve hot or warm.

Serving ($^1/_4$ of casserole) provides: $^3/_4$ Fat, 2$^1/_2$ Vegetables, 1 Protein, $^1/_2$ Bread.

Per Serving: 155 Calories, 5 g Total Fat, 1 g Saturated Fat, 2 mg Cholesterol, 360 mg Sodium, 20 g Total Carbohydrate, 3 g Dietary Fiber, 10 g Protein, 232 mg Calcium.

EGGPLANT TORTA

In Italian, *torta* means cake. When the baked eggplant slices are piled in a circle and covered with tomatoes, herbs, and grated Parmesan cheese, that's just what it looks like.

Makes 4 servings

1 medium eggplant, pared and cut into $^1/_4$" slices

$^3/_4$ cup Tomato-Herb Sauce (page 21), hot

$^3/_4$ ounce Parmesan cheese, grated

$^1/_4$ cup minced fresh basil

1. Preheat oven to 400° F. Spray 2 baking sheets with nonstick cooking spray.
2. Arrange the eggplant slices in a single layer on the baking sheets. Bake 15–20 minutes, until tender.
3. On an 8" plate, arrange one-third of the eggplant slices in a solid circle. Spread $^1/_4$ cup of the sauce over eggplant; sprinkle with one-third of the cheese. Repeat the layers, finishing with the last of the cheese.
4. Sprinkle the top of the torta with the basil. When ready to serve, cut into 4 equal wedges. Place 1 wedge on each of 4 plates and serve.

Serving (1 wedge) provides: $^1/_4$ Fat, 2 Vegetables, $^1/_4$ Protein, 5 Optional Calories.

Per Serving: 85 Calories, 4 g Total Fat, 1 g Saturated Fat, 4 mg Cholesterol, 159 mg Sodium, 10 g Total Carbohydrate, 2 g Dietary Fiber, 4 g Protein, 145 mg Calcium.

11

PIZZAS AND BREADS

POTATO AND SMOKED GOUDA PIZZA

In Italy, tomatoes are a common pizza topping. Although smoked Gouda cheese is less traditional, it complements the potatoes on this slightly unusual but very delicious pizza.

Makes 4 servings

$1^1/_4$ cups + 1 tablespoon all-purpose flour
$1/_4$ ounce rapid-rise active dry yeast (1 envelope)
$1/_2$ teaspoon granulated sugar
$1/_2$ teaspoon salt
$1/_2$ cup hot water (120–130° F)
5 ounces pared all-purpose potato, cut into $1/_8$" slices and dropped into a bowl of cold water

2 teaspoons extra virgin olive oil
$1/_4$ teaspoon coarse salt
3 ounces smoked Gouda cheese, shredded
$1/_4$ teaspoon freshly ground black pepper

1. To prepare the dough, in a large bowl, stir the yeast and sugar into the hot water; let stand 5 minutes, until foamy. Stir in 1 cup of the flour and the salt until a soft dough forms. Sprinkle a work surface with 1 tablespoon of the flour. Turn out the dough onto the prepared work surface and knead 8–10 minutes, working in the remaining $1/_4$ cup flour, until the dough is smooth and elastic.
2. Spray a medium bowl with nonstick cooking spray; place the dough in the bowl and turn to coat all sides. Cover with plastic wrap or a damp towel; let rise in a warm, draft-free place until it doubles in volume, about 30 minutes.
3. Meanwhile, drain the potato; pat dry with paper towels. In a medium bowl, combine the potato, oil and the coarse salt; set aside.
4. Preheat the oven to 425° F. Spray a 12" pizza pan with nonstick cooking spray. Press the dough to cover the pan. Sprinkle with half the cheese and top with the potatoes, arranging them in a single layer. Sprinkle the remaining cheese and the pepper over the potatoes.

5. Bake about 18 minutes, until the crust is crisp and lightly browned. Cut into 8 equal slices and serve.

Serving (2 slices) provides: $^1/_2$ Fat, 1 Protein, 2 Breads.

Per Serving: 283 Calories, 9 g Total Fat, 4 g Saturated Fat, 30 mg Cholesterol, 615 mg Sodium, 39 g Total Carbohydrate, 2 g Dietary Fiber, 11 g Protein, 125 mg Calcium.

QUICK OLIVE PIZZA

Pizza's success often depends on the heat of the oven. Because your oven may take a while to reach 500°F, start preheating it while the dough rises.

Makes 8 servings

1¹/₂ cups all-purpose flour
¹/₄ ounce rapid-rise active dry yeast
  (1 envelope)
¹/₂ teaspoon salt
¹/₂ teaspoon granulated sugar
¹/₂ cup + 2 tablespoons hot water
  (120–130° F)

1 cup prepared pizza-style tomato
  sauce
12 large kalamata olives, pitted and
  chopped

1. To prepare the dough, in a large bowl, stir the yeast and sugar into the hot water; let stand 5 minutes, until foamy. Stir in 1¹/₄ cups of the flour and the salt until a soft dough forms. Sprinkle a work surface with 1 tablespoon of the flour. Turn out the dough onto the prepared work surface and knead 8–10 minutes, working in the remaining 3 tablespoons flour, until the dough is smooth and elastic.

2. Spray a medium bowl with nonstick cooking spray; place the dough in the bowl and turn to coat all sides. Cover with plastic wrap or a damp towel and let rise in a warm, draft-free place until it doubles in volume, about 30 minutes.

3. Preheat the oven to 500° F. Spray a 12" pizza pan with nonstick cooking spray. Press the dough into the pan; pinch up the edges to form a rim.

4. Spoon the sauce evenly over the dough, leaving a 1" border all around; top evenly with the olives. Bake about 10 minutes, until the crust is crisp and lightly browned. Cut into 8 equal slices and serve.

Serving (1 slice) provides: ¹/₄ Fat, ¹/₂ Vegetable, 1 Bread, 10 Optional Calories.

Per Serving: 134 Calories, 3 g Total Fat, 0 g Saturated Fat, 0 mg Cholesterol, 392 mg Sodium, 23 g Total Carbohydrate, 1 g Dietary Fiber, 4 g Protein, 5 mg Calcium.

PIZZERIA PIZZA

On nights when you're craving pizza but still want to avoid excess fat and calories, whip up this authentic pizza.

Makes 8 servings

$^1/_2$ cup + 1 tablespoon warm water (105–115° F)

$^1/_4$ ounce active dry yeast (1 envelope)

$^1/_2$ teaspoon granulated sugar

$1^1/_2$ cups all-purpose flour

1 medium onion, finely chopped

1 tablespoon + 1 teaspoon olive oil

$1^1/_2$ cups canned Italian plum tomatoes (no salt added), drained, chopped, and juice reserved

1 teaspoon dried oregano

$^1/_4$ teaspoon salt

$^3/_4$ ounce Romano cheese, grated

$2^1/_4$ ounces skim-milk mozzarella cheese, shredded

1. To prepare the dough, in a large bowl, stir the yeast and sugar into the hot water; let stand 5 minutes, until foamy. Stir in $1^1/_4$ cups of the flour and the salt until a soft dough forms. Sprinkle a work surface with 1 tablespoon of the flour. Turn out the dough onto the prepared work surface and knead 8–10 minutes, working in the remaining 3 tablespoons flour, until the dough is smooth and elastic.
2. Spray a medium bowl with nonstick cooking spray; place the dough in the bowl and turn to coat all sides. Cover with plastic wrap or a damp towel and let rise in a warm, draft-free place until it doubles in volume, about 1 hour.
3. To prepare the sauce, in a medium saucepan over low heat, combine the onion and oil. Cover and cook 5 minutes. Uncover; add the tomatoes, oregano and salt. Cook, stirring occasionally, 15 minutes more. Set aside and let cool.
4. Spray a 12" pizza pan with nonstick cooking spray. Punch down the dough and press into the pan. Pinch up the edges to form a rim. Cover with a clean kitchen towel; let rise in a warm, draft-free place 30 minutes. Preheat the oven to 500° F.
5. Spread the sauce evenly over dough, leaving a $^1/_2$" border all around. Sprinkle evenly with the Romano and mozzarella cheeses. Bake 10–12 minutes, until the crust is lightly browned and the cheese is melted. Cut into 8 equal slices and serve.

Serving (1 slice) provides: $^1/_2$ Fat, $^1/_2$ Vegetable, $^1/_2$ Protein, 1 Bread.

Per Serving: 146 Calories, 4 g Total Fat, 0 g Saturated Fat, 4 mg Cholesterol, 166 mg Sodium, 22 g Total Carbohydrate, 1 g Dietary Fiber, 7 g Protein, 106 mg Calcium.

Artichoke, Red Pepper and Feta Whole Wheat Pizza

For even more flavor, use feta cheese with cracked black pepper mixed in.

Makes 6 servings

$^1/_2$ cup + 1 tablespoon warm water (105–115° F)

$^1/_4$ ounce active dry yeast (1 envelope)

$^1/_2$ teaspoon granulated sugar

1 cup bread flour

$^1/_2$ cup whole wheat flour

2 cups drained canned or thawed frozen artichoke hearts, chopped

1 medium red bell pepper, seeded and julienned

1 tablespoon olive oil

$^1/_4$ teaspoon salt

$2^1/_4$ ounces feta cheese, crumbled

Freshly ground black pepper, to taste

1. To prepare the dough, in a large bowl, stir the yeast and sugar into the hot water; let stand 5 minutes, until foamy. Stir in the bread flour, $^1/_4$ cup of the whole wheat flour and the salt until a soft dough forms. Sprinkle a work surface with 1 tablespoon of the whole wheat flour. Turn out the dough onto the prepared work surface and knead 8–10 minutes, working in the remaining 3 tablespoons whole wheat flour, until the dough is smooth and elastic.
2. Spray a medium bowl with nonstick cooking spray. Place the dough in the bowl; turn to coat all sides. Cover with plastic wrap or a damp towel and let rise in a warm, draft-free place until it doubles in volume, about 1 hour.
3. Spray a 12" pizza pan with nonstick cooking spray. Punch down the dough and press into the pan; pinch up the edges to form a rim. Cover with a clean towel; let rise in a warm, draft-free place 30 minutes. Preheat the oven to 500° F.
5. In a medium bowl, combine the artichokes, bell pepper, oil and salt. Spoon over the dough; sprinkle with feta cheese and black pepper. Bake about 10 minutes, until the crust is lightly browned. Cut into 6 equal slices and serve.

Serving (1 slice) provides: $^1/_2$ Fat, 1 Vegetable, $^1/_2$ Protein, $1^1/_4$ Breads, 10 Optional Calories.

Per Serving: 197 Calories, 6 g Total Fat, 2 g Saturated Fat, 9 mg Cholesterol, 237 mg Sodium, 30 g Total Carbohydrate, 4 g Dietary Fiber, 8 g Protein, 73 mg Calcium.

THREE-CHEESE PIZZA

Three different cheeses combine to make this pizza taste rich and "cheesy."

Makes 6 servings

1 cup all-purpose flour
$^3/_4$ ounce oat bran
$^1/_4$ ounce active dry yeast (1 envelope)
$^1/_2$ teaspoon granulated sugar
$^1/_2$ teaspoon salt
$^1/_4$ cup + 2 tablespoons hot water
   (120–130° F)

1 tablespoon + 1 teaspoon olive oil
1 cup nonfat ricotta cheese
$^3/_4$ ounce Parmesan cheese, grated
$1^1/_2$ ounces fontina cheese, grated
l large garlic clove, thinly sliced
$^1/_8$ teaspoon salt
Freshly ground black pepper, to taste

1. To prepare the dough, in a large bowl, stir the yeast and sugar into the hot water; let stand 5 minutes, until foamy. Stir in $^3/_4$ cup of the flour, the oat bran, 1 tablespoon of the oil and the salt until a soft dough forms. Sprinkle a work surface with 1 tablespoon of the flour. Turn out the dough onto the prepared work surface and knead 8–10 minutes, working in the remaining 2 tablespoons flour, until the dough is smooth and elastic.
2. Spray a medium bowl with nonstick cooking spray. Place the dough in the bowl and turn to coat all sides. Cover with plastic wrap or a damp towel and let rise in a warm, draft-free place until it doubles in volume, about 1 hour.
3. Spoon the ricotta into a coffee filter or cheesecloth-lined strainer; let drain 15 minutes. Discard liquid in bowl.
4. Preheat the oven to 425° F. Spray a 10" pizza pan with nonstick cooking spray. Punch down the dough and press the dough into the pan; pinch up the edges to form a rim. Spread the ricotta evenly over the dough, leaving a $^1/_2$" border all around. Sprinkle evenly with the Parmesan, fontina, garlic, salt and pepper; drizzle evenly with the remaining teaspoon oil. Bake about 18 minutes, until the crust is lightly browned. Cut into 6 equal slices and serve.

Serving (1 slice) provides: 1 Fat, $1^1/_2$ Proteins, $1^1/_2$ Breads.

Per Serving: 209 Calories, 11 g Total Fat, 5 g Saturated Fat, 28 mg Cholesterol, 402 mg Sodium, 20 g Total Carbohydrate, 1 g Dietary Fiber, 10 g Protein, 169 mg Calcium.

PARMESAN FOCACCIA

Focaccia is basically pizza dough with ingredients mixed in or, sometimes, sprinkled on top. In fact, the first pizzas sold in America didn't have the thin Neapolitan-style crust, but the thicker focaccia.

Makes 24 servings

1 1/2 cups warm water (105–115° F)
1/4 ounce active dry yeast (1 envelope)
1 teaspoon granulated sugar
2 tablespoons olive oil
4 1/2 cups all-purpose flour
1 1/2 teaspoons dried oregano
1 teaspoon salt
1 1/2 ounces Parmesan cheese, grated

1. To prepare the dough by hand, in a large bowl, combine 1/2 cup of the water and the yeast; stir in the sugar. Let stand 10 minutes, until foamy. Stir in 1 tablespoon of the oil and the remaining 1 cup water. Add 4 cups of the flour, the oregano and salt; stir to form a soft dough.
2. If using a food processor, in a small bowl, combine 1/2 cup of the water and the yeast; stir in the sugar. Let stand 10 minutes, until foamy. In the food processor, combine 4 cups of the flour, the oregano and salt. With the machine running, pour in the yeast mixture, oil and remaining 1 cup water. When the dough gathers into a ball, process 40 seconds to knead.
3. Sprinkle a work surface with 1 tablespoon of the remaining flour; turn out the dough onto the prepared work surface and knead about 10 minutes (if using a food processor, knead by hand just 1 minute), adding all but 1 teaspoon of the remaining flour as needed, until the dough is smooth and elastic.
4. Flour a gallon-size sealable plastic bag with the remaining 1 teaspoon flour; place the dough in the bag. Refrigerate overnight, until it doubles in volume.
5. Spray a 15 × 10 × 1" jelly-roll pan with nonstick cooking spray. Press the dough evenly into the corners of the pan (the dough is elastic so keep stretching it). Cover with a clean towel; let rise in a warm, draft-free place 30 minutes.
6. Arrange the oven racks to divide the oven in half. Preheat the oven to 450° F.
7. Brush the remaining 1 tablespoon oil over the dough. Bake in the center of the oven 10 minutes; reduce the heat to 400° F. Sprinkle evenly with the cheese; bake about 15 minutes more, until crisp and browned. Cut into 24 equal pieces.

Serving (one 1-ounce piece) provides: 1/4 Fat, 1 Bread, 5 Optional Calories.

Per Serving: 105 Calories, 2 g Total Fat, 1 g Saturated Fat, 1 mg Cholesterol, 125 mg Sodium, 18 g Total Carbohydrate, 1 g Dietary Fiber, 3 g Protein, 30 mg Calcium.

BREADSTICKS

Vary the herbs—or even substitute Parmesan cheese—for variations on this basic recipe.

Makes 24 servings

³/₄ cup warm water (105–115° F)
¹/₄ ounce active dry yeast (1 envelope)
¹/₂ teaspoon granulated sugar
2³/₄ cups + 2 tablespoons bread flour*

1 tablespoon dried rosemary leaves, crumbled
1 teaspoon salt
2 tablespoons olive oil

1. Pour the warm water into a large bowl; sprinkle with the yeast and sugar. Let stand 10 minutes, until foamy.
2. In a medium bowl, combine 2¹/₄ cups of the flour, the rosemary and salt. Stir the flour mixture and the oil into the yeast mixture until the dough forms a ball. Sprinkle 1 tablespoon of the remaining flour on a work surface; knead the dough 8–10 minutes, adding 1 tablespoon flour at a time, until the dough is no longer sticky and is smooth and elastic.
3. Sprinkle the reserved 2 tablespoons flour on a large cutting board. Place the dough on the board and roll into a 10 × 6" rectangle. Cover with a clean kitchen towel and let rise in a warm, draft-free place until it doubles in volume, about 1 hour.
4. Preheat the oven to 450° F. Spray 2 baking sheets with nonstick cooking spray.
5. With a pizza cutter or long sharp knife, cut the dough cross-wise into 4 equal parts, then cut each part lengthwise into 6 equal strips, to make a total of 24 strips. Roll each strip into a ¹/₂" rope. Pull and stretch each rope and place on the prepared pan about 1" apart (the ropes will shrink to approximately 8" lengths). Repeat with the remaining dough, keeping the unstretched dough covered with the towel. Bake about 18 minutes, until golden. Cool completely on a wire rack. Store in an airtight container.

Serving: (1 breadstick) provides: ¹/₄ Fat, ¹/₂ Bread, 10 Optional Calories.

Per Serving: 71 Calories, 2 g Total Fat, 0 g Saturated Fat, 0 mg Cholesterol, 92 mg Sodium, 12 g Total Carbohydrate, 0 g Dietary Fiber, 2 g Protein, 5 mg Calcium.

*Reserve 2 tablespoons flour.

CHEESE STICKS

These delectable sticks are a nice accompaniment to a hearty soup or fresh salad.

Makes 8 servings

2 tablespoons all-purpose flour	1 teaspoon dried thyme leaves
One 10-ounce package refrigerator	1/4 teaspoon ground red pepper
pizza dough	Freshly ground black pepper,
1 1/2 ounces Parmesan cheese, grated	to taste
2 teaspoons dried rosemary leaves	

1. Preheat the oven to 400° F. Spray 2 baking sheets with nonstick cooking spray.
2. Sprinkle a clean work surface with 1 tablespoon of the flour. Turn out the dough onto the prepared work surface and roll into an 18 × 11" rectangle. Sprinkle one-half of the dough evenly with the cheese, rosemary, thyme, and red and black peppers; fold over the other side of dough, like a book, to form a 9 × 11" rectangle. Sprinkle evenly with the remaining tablespoon flour.
3. Roll dough several times to press in the filling and create a 10 × 12" rectangle. Cut the dough in half lengthwise, creating two 5 × 12" rectangles; along the short seams, cut the dough into 1/2" strips. Twist each strip 6 or 7 times and place on the prepared baking sheet, pressing the ends into the pan to hold the twist in place. Repeat to make 48 sticks. Bake about 15 minutes, until golden brown. Cool slightly on a wire rack and serve warm. Store any leftovers in an airtight container.

Serving (6 sticks) provides: 1/4 Protein, 1 1/4 Breads, 10 Optional Calories.

Per Serving: 125 Calories, 3 g Total Fat, 1 g Saturated Fat, 4 mg Cholesterol, 294 mg Sodium, 18 g Total Carbohydrate, 1 g Dietary Fiber, 5 g Protein, 80 mg Calcium.

SEMOLINA BREAD

Although it may seem a strange thing to do, be sure to spray the bread and the inside of the oven with water—it's the secret to a crisp crust. Semolina, a coarsely ground wheat flour, is available at health food and Italian specialty food stores.

Makes 14 servings

$^1/_4$ ounce active-dry yeast (1 envelope)
$^1/_2$ teaspoon granulated sugar
1 cup + 1 tablespoon warm water (105–115° F)
2 cups + 1 tablespoon bread flour

1 cup semolina flour*
1 teaspoon salt
2 teaspoons olive oil
1 tablespoon cornmeal
1 tablespoon sesame seeds

1. In a small bowl, stir the yeast and sugar into the warm water; let stand 10 minutes, until foamy.
2. In a food processor, combine 2 cups of the bread flour, the semolina flour and salt. With the machine running, add the yeast mixture and oil. Pulse until the dough gathers into a ball; process 40 seconds more to knead.
3. Spray a large bowl with nonstick cooking spray; place the dough in the bowl, turning to coat all sides. Cover with plastic wrap or a damp towel and let rise in a warm, draft-free place until it doubles in volume, about $1^1/_2$ hours.
4. Sprinkle a baking sheet with the cornmeal; set aside. Sprinkle a work surface with the remaining 1 tablespoon flour. Punch down the dough; turn out the dough onto the prepared work surface and knead briefly. Roll into a 2" rope. Coil the rope into an inverted "S" shape and place on the prepared baking sheet. Cover loosely with a clean kitchen towel and let rise in a warm, draft-free place until it doubles in volume, 1–$1^1/_2$ hours.
5. Arrange the oven racks to divide the oven in half. Preheat the oven to 425° F.
6. Spray the loaf with water and sprinkle evenly with sesame seeds. Place on middle rack in the oven. Spray the walls of the oven with water and close the oven door. After 30 seconds, spray the walls of the oven again. Bake 30 minutes, until the crust is golden and an instant-read thermometer reaches 200–210° F. Remove the bread from the baking sheet and cool slightly on a wire rack; cut into 14 equal slices.

Serving (one $^1/_2$-ounce slice) provides: 1 Bread, 25 Optional Calories.

Per Serving: 130 Calories, 2 g Total Fat, 0 g Saturated Fat, 0 mg Cholesterol, 158 mg Sodium, 24 g Total Carbohydrate, 1 g Dietary Fiber, 4 g Protein, 13 mg Calcium.

GARLIC KNOTS

Though perhaps not authentically Italian, these savory rolls, redolent of garlic, are a perfect example of Italian-American ingenuity.

Makes 8 servings

1 pound thawed frozen pizza
  dough
2 tablespoons all-purpose flour

1 tablespoon + 1 teaspoon olive oil
2 large garlic cloves, minced
$^1/_4$ teaspoon coarse salt

1. Spray a large bowl with nonstick cooking spray. Place the dough in the prepared bowl and turn to coat all sides. Cover with plastic wrap or a damp towel and let rise in a warm, draft-free place, until it doubles in volume, about 1 hour.
2. Preheat the oven to 375° F. Spray a baking sheet with nonstick cooking spray.
3. Divide the dough into eight equal pieces. Sprinkle a work surface with the flour. Roll each piece of dough to an 8" length and tie into a knot. Place on the prepared baking sheet. Bake 35 minutes, until golden brown. Cool on a wire rack 10–15 minutes.
4. In a small nonstick skillet over low heat, combine the oil and garlic; cook 3 minutes, until the garlic is barely golden. Brush the mixture evenly over each knot and sprinkle evenly with the salt. Serve immediately.

Serving (1 garlic knot) provides: $^1/_2$ Fat, 2 Breads, 10 Optional Calories.

Per Serving: 174 Calories, 5 g Total Fat, 1 g Saturated Fat, 0 mg Cholesterol, 357 mg Sodium, 28 g Total Carbohydrate, 1 g Dietary Fiber, 5 g Protein, 2 mg Calcium.

12

DESSERTS

Lemon Sorbet

Espresso Granita

Gelato Affogato

Orange Panna Cotta

Tiramisu

Budino di Ricotta

Layered Polenta Cake

Italian Cheesecake

Chocolate Grappa Cake

Pumpkin-Pistachio Biscotti

Spiced Pears

Roasted Pears with Cannoli Cream

Pine Nut–Filled Figs with Chocolate Icing

Amaretti-Stuffed Peaches

Strawberries in Balsamic Vinegar

LEMON SORBET

In Southern Italy, lemon trees grow everywhere. As a result, lemons are a popular ingredient. This refreshing dessert evokes the land and its foods.

Makes 12 servings

1 cup granulated sugar
1 teaspoon grated lemon zest*

1 cup fresh lemon juice

1. Place the sugar in a medium saucepan; add 4 cups water; bring to a boil. Reduce the heat to low; simmer, stirring occasionally, 3 minutes, until the sugar is dissolved. Remove from the heat and stir in the zest and juice. Cool 30 minutes; refrigerate, covered, at least 3 hours or overnight.
2. Transfer the mixture to an ice cream freezer and freeze according to the manufacturer's instructions. Divide evenly among 12 bowls and serve.

Serving (¹/₂ cup) provides: 60 Optional Calories.

Per Serving: 70 Calories, 0 g Total Fat, 0 g Saturated Fat, 0 mg Cholesterol, 0 mg Sodium, 18 g Total Carbohydrate, 0 g Dietary Fiber, 0 g Protein, 2 mg Calcium.

The zest of the lemon is the peel without any of the pith (white membrane). To remove zest from lemon, use a zester or the fine side of a vegetable grater.

ESPRESSO GRANITA

Granitas have a coarser, grainier texture than sorbets. If you prefer a smoother dessert, omit step 3 and prepare the espresso mixture in your ice cream maker.

Makes 7 servings

2 cups brewed decaffeinated espresso or dark roast coffee, chilled

$^1/_3$ cup granulated sugar
2 teaspoons lemon zest*

1. Freeze a 9" square metal baking pan overnight.
2. In a medium bowl, whisk the espresso and sugar until the sugar is dissolved; add the zest.
3. Pour the espresso mixture into the baking pan. Freeze about 2 hours, stirring with a fork every 20 minutes, until the mixture is evenly frozen but still grainy. Cover with foil and keep frozen until ready to serve.

Serving ($^1/_2$ cup) provides: 35 Optional Calories.

Per Serving: 38 Calories, 0 g Total Fat, 0 g Saturated Fat, 0 mg Cholesterol, 1 mg Sodium, 10 g Total Carbohydrate, 0 g Dietary Fiber, 0 g Protein, 2 mg Calcium.

*The zest of the lemon is the peel without any of the pith (white membrane). To remove zest from lemon, use a zester or the fine side of a vegetable grater; wrap lemon in plastic wrap and refrigerate for later use.

GELATO AFFOGATO

DROWNED FROZEN YOGURT

By pouring hot espresso over frozen yogurt, this becomes a coffee float in a dish.

Makes 4 servings

1 tablespoon slivered lemon zest*
1 teaspoon granulated sugar
16 fluid ounces (2 cups) sugar-free
  vanilla or coffee nonfat frozen
  yogurt

$^1/_2$ cup hot brewed decaffeinated
  espresso coffee

1. Place the lemon zest in a small saucepan; add $^1/_4$ cup water. Bring to a boil; remove from heat and let stand 10 minutes. Drain the zest and pat dry with a paper towel. Place the zest in a single layer on wax paper and sprinkle evenly with the sugar; let stand 30 minutes.
2. Scoop $^3/_4$ cup frozen yogurt into each of 4 dessert dishes; pour 2 tablespoons espresso over each. Garnish each portion with one-fourth of the zest and any remaining sugar. Serve immediately.

Serving ($^1/_2$ cup) provides: $^1/_4$ Milk, 55 Optional Calories.

Per Serving: 56 Calories, 0 g Total Fat, 0 g Saturated Fat, 2 mg Cholesterol, 66 mg Sodium, 10 g Total Carbohydrate, 0 g Dietary Fiber, 5 g Protein, 153 mg Calcium.

---

*The zest of the lemon is the peel without any of the pith (white membrane). To remove zest from lemon, use a zester or the fine side of a vegetable grater; wrap lemon in plastic wrap and refrigerate for later use.

ORANGE PANNA COTTA

COOKED "CREAM"

Traditionally made with eggs, this classic dessert is a fat and cholesterol minefield. By using gelatin instead, we lower the fat and cholesterol without sacrificing flavor.

Makes 4 servings

2 cups lowfat (1%) milk
$^1/_4$ ounce unflavored gelatin
   (1 envelope)
$^1/_4$ cup granulated sugar
1 teaspoon vanilla extract
1 teaspoon orange extract

1 teaspoon grated orange zest*
Pinch salt
$^1/_2$ cup frozen light whipped
   topping (10 calories per
   tablespoon)
Ground cinnamon

1. In a medium nonstick saucepan, combine the milk and gelatin; let stand about 5 minutes, until the gelatin softens.
2. Place the milk mixture over low heat, stirring until the gelatin is completely dissolved, about 5 minutes.
3. Whisk in the sugar, vanilla and orange extracts, zest and salt; bring to a simmer, stirring frequently. Pour evenly into four $^1/_2$-cup ramekins. Cool slightly; refrigerate, covered, overnight. To serve, top each with 2 tablespoons whipped topping and a sprinkling of cinnamon.

Serving ($^1/_2$ cup) provides: $^1/_2$ Milk, 60 Optional Calories.

Per Serving: 134 Calories, 2 g Total Fat, 2 g Saturated Fat, 5 mg Cholesterol, 96 mg Sodium, 21 g Total Carbohydrate, 0 g Dietary Fiber, 5 g Protein, 152 mg Calcium.

The zest of the orange is the peel without any of the pith (white membrane). To remove zest from orange , use a zester or the fine side of a vegetable grater; wrap orange in plastic wrap and refrigerate for later use.

TIRAMISU

Since these egg whites are not cooked, use salmonella-negative powdered egg whites (available in the baking section of many supermarkets) for food safety. To get the most volume when you beat the egg whites, make sure the stainless steel bowl and the beaters are very clean and completely dry.

Makes 8 servings

$^1/_4$ cup cooled brewed decaffeinated espresso or strong decaffeinated black coffee

12 ladyfinger biscuits (3" long)

$^1/_2$ cup lukewarm water (105–115° F)

2 tablespoons + 2 teaspoons powdered egg whites

$1^1/_3$ cups nonfat ricotta cheese

$^1/_3$ cup fat-free egg substitute

$^1/_2$ cup mascarpone cheese

2 tablespoons granulated sugar

2 teaspoons unsweetened cocoa powder

1. Pour the espresso into a wide shallow bowl. Dip each biscuit into the espresso and place in a single layer in an 8" square glass or ceramic baking dish; set aside.
2. In a clean large stainless steel bowl, combine the lukewarm water and powdered egg whites; stir slowly, 3–4 minutes, until dissolved. With an electric mixer with dry beaters, beat at medium-high speed, 5–7 minutes, until stiff peaks form.
3. In a large bowl, beat together the ricotta, egg substitute, mascarpone and sugar. Gently fold in the beaten whites; pour over the ladyfingers. Cover and refrigerate 6–8 hours. Just before serving, sprinkle with the cocoa. Divide evenly among 8 plates and serve.

Serving ($^3/_4$ cup) provides: 1 Protein, 95 Optional Calories.

Per Serving: 182 Calories, 8 g Total Fat, 0 g Saturated Fat, 80 mg Cholesterol, 117 mg Sodium, 15 g Total Carbohydrate, 0 g Dietary Fiber, 10 g Protein, 213 mg Calcium.

BUDINO DI RICOTTA

ALMOND-RICOTTA PUDDING

This old-fashioned dessert is a cross between a flan and a soufflé.

Makes 8 servings

2 cups part-skim ricotta cheese
8 amaretti cookies (1" diameter), crushed
4 eggs, separated (at room temperature)
$^{1}/_{4}$ cup cornstarch
1 fluid ounce (2 tablespoons) amaretto liqueur
$^{1}/_{8}$ teaspoon cream of tartar
$^{1}/_{4}$ cup granulated sugar

1. Arrange the racks to divide the oven in half. Preheat the oven to 375° F. Spray a 6-cup soufflé dish with nonstick cooking spray.
2. In a large bowl, combine the ricotta, cookies, egg yolks, cornstarch and amaretto; set aside.
3. In a medium bowl with an electric mixer at high speed, beat the egg whites with the cream of tartar until foamy. Gradually beat in the sugar, 1 table-spoon at a time, until the whites are stiff and glossy but not dry. Gently fold the egg whites, one-third at a time, into the ricotta mixture until no white streaks remain.
4. Spoon the batter into the prepared dish. Place the soufflé dish in a 13 × 9" baking dish; place on the center oven rack. Pour boiling water into the bak-ing dish to come halfway up the side of the soufflé dish. Bake 45 minutes, until puffed and golden. Divide evenly among 8 plates and serve warm.

Serving ($^{3}/_{4}$ cup) provides: $^{3}/_{4}$ Fat, 2 Proteins, 85 Optional Calories.

Per Serving: 198 Calories, 8 g Total Fat, 4 g Saturated Fat, 125 mg Cholesterol, 111 mg Sodium, 19 g Total Carbohydrate, 0 g Dietary Fiber, 10 g Protein, 180 mg Calcium.

LAYERED POLENTA CAKE

Use your favorite flavor of spreadable fruit in this cake. Make sure the bowl and beaters are clean and dry before you start beating the egg whites—any fat or moisture can reduce their volume.

Makes 8 servings

1 cup yellow cornmeal
$^3/_4$ cup self-rising cake flour
1 teaspoon baking soda
$^1/_4$ teaspoon salt
$^2/_3$ cup granulated sugar
3 eggs, separated (at room
   temperature)

$^1/_4$ cup low-fat (1%) buttermilk
4 teaspoons vegetable oil
2 teaspoons vanilla extract
$^1/_2$ cup spreadable fruit
2 teaspoons confectioners sugar

1. Preheat the oven to 350° F. Spray an 8" springform pan with nonstick cooking spray.
2. In a large bowl, combine the cornmeal, flour, baking soda and salt.
3. In a medium bowl with an electric mixer at medium-high speed, cream $^1/_3$ cup of the sugar and the egg yolks about 5 minutes, until light and fluffy. Add the buttermilk, oil and vanilla and beat 1 minute more. Beat the egg yolk mixture into the cornmeal mixture.
4. In a medium-sized stainless steel bowl with dry beaters, beat the egg whites at high speed until foamy. Gradually beat in the remaining $^1/_3$ cup sugar, 1 tablespoon or so at a time, until the whites are stiff and glossy but not dry. Gently fold the egg whites, one-third at a time, into the cornmeal mixture, until no white streaks remain.
5. Spoon the batter into the prepared pan. Bake 40 minutes, until the center is puffed and golden and a toothpick inserted in the center comes out clean. Cool on a wire rack in the pan 10 minutes. Run a sharp knife around the inside of the pan to release the cake. Remove the ring; cool completely on rack.
6. With a long serrated knife, cut the cake in half. Place the bottom half on a platter and spread with the spreadable fruit; cover with the top half and sprinkle evenly with confectioners sugar. Cut into 8 equal wedges and serve.

Serving (1 wedge) provides: $^1/_2$ Fat, 1 Fruit, $^1/_4$ Protein, $1^1/_2$ Breads, 75 Optional Calories.

Per Serving: 266 Calories, 5 g Total Fat, 1 g Saturated Fat, 80 mg Cholesterol, 384 mg Sodium, 50 g Total Carbohydrate, 1 g Dietary Fiber, 5 g Protein, 21 mg Calcium.

ITALIAN CHEESECAKE

American-style cheesecake gets its light yet rich texture from cream cheese. The Italian version of this classic dessert uses ricotta cheese—it's denser, like a flourless cake.

Makes 12 servings

12 graham crackers (2¹/₂" squares)
3 cups part-skim ricotta cheese
¹/₂ cup nonfat cream cheese
¹/₂ cup granulated sugar
¹/₄ cup cornstarch

2 teaspoons grated orange zest*
4 eggs
1¹/₂ tablespoons dark rum
2 teaspoons vanilla extract

1. Preheat the oven to 300° F. Spray an 8" springform pan with nonstick cooking spray. In a gallon-size sealable plastic bag, crush the graham crackers to fine crumbs. Sprinkle the crumbs into the bottom of the prepared pan and pat down evenly.
2. In a food processor, combine the ricotta and cream cheeses; sift the sugar and cornstarch onto cheese mixture and add the zest. Process about 20 seconds more, until smooth.
3. In a small bowl, combine the eggs, rum and vanilla. With the food processor running, add the egg mixture. Process about 10 seconds, until combined, scraping down the sides of the bowl as needed. Pour the batter into the prepared pan.
4. Bake 1¹/₂–2 hours, until golden and puffed and a knife inserted in the center comes out clean. Cool on a wire rack in the pan 1 hour. Run a sharp knife around the inside of the pan to release the cheesecake. Remove the ring; cool 1 hour more. Wrap in foil and refrigerate overnight. Cut into 8 equal slices and serve.

Serving (1 slice) provides: 1¹/₄ Proteins, ¹/₄ Bread, 65 Optional Calories.

Per Serving: 198 Calories, 7 g Total Fat, 4 g Saturated Fat, 91 mg Cholesterol, 186 mg Sodium, 20 g Total Carbohydrate, 0 g Dietary Fiber, 11 g Protein, 204 mg Calcium.

*The zest of the orange is the peel without any of the pith (white membrane). To remove zest from orange, use a zester or the fine side of a vegetable grater; wrap orange in plastic wrap and refrigerate for later use.

CHOCOLATE GRAPPA CAKE

This cake is actually better the next day. If you prefer, substitute Frangelico or Amaretto for the *grappa* (Italian brandy).

Makes 12 servings

6 tablespoons raisins
2 fluid ounces ($^1/_4$ cup) grappa
  (Italian brandy)
5 tablespoons unsalted margarine,
  at room temperature
1 cup + 2 tablespoons +
  2 teaspoons granulated sugar
$^2/_3$ cup fat-free egg substitute
1 teaspoon vanilla extract

$2^1/_4$ cups all-purpose flour
$^1/_3$ cup unsweetened cocoa powder
$^3/_4$ teaspoon baking powder
$^1/_2$ teaspoon baking soda
$^1/_4$ teaspoon cinnamon
$^1/_4$ teaspoon salt
1 cup aspartame-sweetened vanilla
  nonfat yogurt

1. In a small bowl, soak the raisins in the grappa 30 minutes. Drain the raisins, reserving the grappa separately; set aside.
2. Arrange the oven racks to divide the oven in half. Preheat the oven to 350° F. Spray an $8^1/_2 \times 4^1/_2$" loaf pan with nonstick cooking spray.
3. In a large bowl with an electric mixer at medium speed, cream the margarine; gradually add $^2/_3$ cup of the sugar and continue beating 5 minutes, until light and fluffy. Beat in the egg substitute and vanilla.
4. In a medium bowl, combine the flour, cocoa, baking powder, baking soda, cinnamon and salt. With the mixer at low speed, add the flour mixture to the margarine mixture alternately with the yogurt, beginning and ending with the flour mixture. Fold in the raisins.
5. Spoon the batter into the prepared pan. Bake about 1 hour, until a toothpick inserted in the center comes out clean. Cool on a wire rack in the pan 15 minutes. Run a knife around the inside of the pan to release the cake, but do not remove.

6. To prepare the syrup, in a small saucepan, combine the remaining $^1/_2$ cup sugar with $^1/_3$ cup of water; bring to a boil over high heat; boil, without stirring, 1 minute. Remove from the heat; stir in the reserved grappa. Pierce the cake in several places with a skewer or long meat fork. Pour the grappa syrup slowly over the cake until it is absorbed. Cool the cake completely. When ready to serve, remove the cake from the pan and cut into 12 equal slices.

Serving (1 slice) provides: $1^1/_4$ Fats, $^1/_4$ Fruit, 1 Bread, 110 Optional Calories.

Per Serving: 251 Calories, 5 g Total Fat, 1 g Saturated Fat, 0 mg Cholesterol, 163 mg Sodium, 44 g Total Carbohydrate, 2 g Dietary Fiber, 5 g Protein, 57 mg Calcium.

PUMPKIN-PISTACHIO BISCOTTI

These crunchy treats can be stored up to a month in an airtight container—they also freeze well.

Makes 16 servings

$^2/_3$ cup canned pumpkin purée
$^1/_4$ cup granulated sugar
2 eggs
2 teaspoons orange zest*
1 teaspoon vanilla extract
$^1/_4$ teaspoon almond extract
  (optional)

$2^1/_4$ cups all-purpose flour
$1^1/_2$ teaspoons baking powder
$^1/_4$ teaspoon ground nutmeg
Pinch salt
2 ounces shelled unsalted roasted
  pistachios, coarsely chopped

1. Preheat the oven to 325° F. Line 2 baking sheets with wax paper or parchment and spray evenly with nonstick cooking spray.
2. In a large bowl, combine the pumpkin and sugar; whisk in the eggs, orange zest, vanilla and almond extracts (if using).
3. In a medium bowl, combine the flour, baking powder, nutmeg and salt; sprinkle over the pumpkin mixture; stir gently to blend. Stir in the pistachios. Divide dough in half.
4. Shape each dough half into a 12 × 2" log along the center of each prepared baking sheet. Bake until lightly browned, 25 minutes. Remove from the baking sheets; cool on wire racks 5 minutes, leaving the oven on.
5. Place the baked logs on a cutting board and cut with a serrated knife into $^1/_4$" slices, to make 64 biscotti. Place the slices flat on the baking sheets and return to the oven, turning once, until slightly dried, 10 minutes. Cool completely on wire racks and store in an airtight container.

Serving (4 biscotti) provides: $^1/_4$ Fat, $^1/_4$ Protein, $^3/_4$ Bread, 10 Optional Calories.

Per Serving: 112 Calories, 3 g Total Fat, 0 g Saturated Fat, 27 mg Total Cholesterol, 63 mg Sodium, 18 g Total Carbohydrate, 1 g Dietary Fiber, 3 g Protein, 39 mg Calcium.

---

* The zest of the orange is the peel without any of the pith (white membrane). To remove zest from orange, use a zester or the fine side of a vegetable grater; wrap orange in plastic wrap and refrigerate for later use.

SPICED PEARS

These brilliant red pears are a delicious way to get more fresh fruit in your diet.

Makes 4 servings

4 small Bosc or Anjou pears, pared
1 tablespoon fresh lemon juice
1 cup low-calorie cranberry juice
  cocktail

$1/4$ cup granulated sugar
6 whole cloves
One 3" cinnamon stick

1. Preheat the oven to 450° F.
2. Place the pears in a baking dish to fit snugly; sprinkle with the lemon juice.
3. In a small bowl, combine the cranberry juice, sugar and cloves. Pour evenly over the pears; add the cinnamon stick to the dish.
4. Bake, basting the pears every 5–10 minutes, 45 minutes, until the pears are tender when pierced with a fork. Cool on a wire rack in the pan 30 minutes, continuing to baste every 5–10 minutes.
5. Remove and discard the cloves and cinnamon stick. If necessary, trim a small slice from the bottom of the pears so they stand upright. Place 1 pear on each of 4 plates; spoon 2 tablespoons of the liquid over each pear and serve.

Serving (1 pear with 2 tablespoons liquid) provides: $1^{1}/4$ Fruits, 45 Optional Calories.

Per Serving: 154 Calories, 1 g Total Fat, 0 g Saturated Fat, 0 mg Cholesterol, 2 mg Sodium, 39 g Total Carbohydrate, 4 g Dietary Fiber, 1 g Protein, 27 mg Calcium.

ROASTED PEARS WITH CANNOLI CREAM

Both the pears and cannoli cream may be prepared and refrigerated, separately, overnight. To serve, bring to room temperature, then fill the pears and serve immediately.

Makes 4 servings

1 cup part-skim ricotta cheese
1/2 teaspoon cinnamon
4 firm ripe small Bosc pears, cored and halved (do not pare)

1/4 cup confectioners sugar
1/2 teaspoon vanilla extract
1/2 ounce (1 tablespoon) mini chocolate chips

1. Spoon the ricotta into a coffee filter or cheesecloth-lined strainer; place over a bowl. Refrigerate, covered, 2 hours. Discard the liquid in the bowl.
2. Preheat the oven to 425° F. Spray an 11 × 7" baking dish with nonstick cooking spray.
3. Sprinkle 1/4 teaspoon of the cinnamon evenly over the cut sides of the pears; place the pears, cut-side down, in the prepared dish. Roast 30 minutes. Cool on a wire rack in the pan for 30 minutes.
4. To prepare the cannoli cream, in a medium bowl with a fork or small whisk, or in a mini food processor, combine the ricotta, sugar, the remaining 1/4 teaspoon cinnamon and the vanilla until well blended. Fold in the chips. Let stand, covered, 30 minutes at room temperature. Spoon one heaping tablespoon into each pear half; place 2 halves on each of 4 plates and serve at once.

Serving (2 pear halves with 1 generous tablespoon cannoli cream) provides: 1 Fruit, 1 Protein, 65 Optional Calories.

Per Serving: 227 Calories, 7 g Total Fat, 4 g Saturated Fat, 19 mg Cholesterol, 77 mg Sodium, 37 g Total Carbohydrate, 4 g Dietary Fiber, 8 g Protein, 189 mg Calcium.

PINE NUT–FILLED FIGS WITH CHOCOLATE ICING

Pine nuts are a savory filling for the sweet figs.

Makes 4 servings

4 large dried figs	1 ounce semisweet chocolate,
4 teaspoons pine nuts	chopped

1. Preheat the oven to 350° F.
2. Trim the stems from the figs; cut each almost in half crosswise (do not separate halves). Gently open figs and press 1 teaspoon pine nuts into each fig; press to close. Carefully place figs in an 8" square baking pan; bake 15 minutes, until the figs are slightly darkened and the nuts are toasted.
3. In a small saucepan over low heat, melt the chocolate, stirring frequently. Spread the top of each fig with an equal amount of chocolate. Let stand at room temperature 2 hours, until the chocolate is set, or refrigerate 20 minutes to set quickly.

Serving (1 fig) provides: $^{1}/_{4}$ Fat, 1 Fruit, 45 Optional Calories.

Per Serving: 103 Calories, 4 g Total Fat, 2 g Saturated Fat, 0 mg Cholesterol, 3 mg Sodium, 19 g Total Carbohydrate, 2 g Dietary Fiber, 2 g Protein, 34 mg Calcium.

AMARETTI-STUFFED PEACHES

Make sure your peaches aren't too soft—if they feel firm but yield to gentle pressure around the stem, they're just right.

Makes 6 servings

6 ripe but firm medium peaches, halved and pitted
6 amaretti cookies (1" diameter), crushed
1 tablespoon granulated sugar
1 egg white
1 1/2 teaspoons unsalted whipped butter

1. Preheat the oven to 375° F. Spray a 9" square baking pan with nonstick cooking spray.
2. With a grapefruit spoon, scoop some pulp from each peach half to make a deep well. Chop the pulp and place in a small bowl. Place the peach halves, cut-side up, in the prepared pan.
3. Add the cookies, sugar and egg white to the reserved pulp, stirring until combined. Spoon the mixture evenly into each peach half and dot each with 1/4 teaspoon of the butter. Bake 30 minutes, until bubbling. Serve warm or at room temperature.

Serving (2 stuffed peach halves) provides: 3/4 Fat, 1 Fruit, 1/2 Protein, 50 Optional Calories.

Per Serving: 97 Calories, 1 g Total Fat, 0 g Saturated Fat, 2 mg Cholesterol, 12 mg Sodium, 21 g Total Carbohydrate, 2 g Dietary Fiber, 2 g Protein, 7 mg Calcium.

STRAWBERRIES IN BALSAMIC VINEGAR

Pungent balsamic vinegar really brings out the essence of the berries in this refreshing sweet-and-sour dessert.

Makes 4 servings

3 cups hulled whole strawberries, halved

1 tablespoon granulated sugar
2 teaspoons balsamic vinegar

1. In a medium bowl, combine the strawberries and sugar. Cover and refrigerate 2 hours, until syrupy.
2. Stir the vinegar into the strawberry mixture and let stand 30 minutes at room temperature. Divide evenly among 4 bowls and serve.

Serving (³/₄ cup) provides: ³/₄ Fruit, 10 Optional Calories.

Per Serving: 47 Calories, 0 g Total Fat, 0 g Saturated Fat, 0 mg Cholesterol, 1 mg Sodium, 11 g Total Carbohydrate, 3 g Dietary Fiber, 1 g Protein, 16 mg Calcium.

METRIC CONVERSIONS

If you are converting the recipes in this book to metric measurements, use the following chart as a guide.

Volume		Weight		Length		Oven Temperatures	
1/4 teaspoon	1 milliliter	1 ounce	30 grams	1 inch	25 millimeters	250°F	120°C
1/2 teaspoon	2 milliliters	1/4 pound	120 grams	1 inch	2.5 centimeters	275°F	140°C
1 teaspoon	5 milliliters	1/2 pound	240 grams			300°F	150°C
1 tablespoon	15 milliliters	3/4 pound	360 grams			325°F	160°C
2 tablespoons	30 milliliters	1 pound	480 grams			350°F	180°C
3 tablespoons	45 milliliters					375°F	190°C
1/4 cup	50 milliliters					400°F	200°C
1/3 cup	75 milliliters					425°F	220°C
1/2 cup	125 milliliters					450°F	230°C
2/3 cup	150 milliliters					475°F	250°C
3/4 cup	175 milliliters					500°F	260°C
1 cup	250 milliliters					525°F	270°C
1 quart	1 liter						

DRY AND LIQUID MEASUREMENT EQUIVALENTS

Teaspoons	Tablespoons	Cups	Fluid Ounces
3 teaspoons	1 tablespoon		1/2 fluid ounce
6 teaspoons	2 tablespoons	1/8 cup	1 fluid ounce
8 teaspoons	2 tablespoons plus 2 teaspoons	1/6 cup	
12 teaspoons	4 tablespoons	1/4 cup	2 fluid ounces
15 teaspoons	5 tablespoons	1/3 cup minus 1 teaspoon	
16 teaspoons	5 tablespoons plus 1 teaspoon	1/3 cup	
18 teaspoons	6 tablespoons	1/3 cup plus two teaspoons	3 fluid ounces
24 teaspoons	8 tablespoons	1/2 cup	4 fluid ounces
30 teaspoons	10 tablespoons	1/2 cup plus 2 tablespoons	5 fluid ounces
32 teaspoons	10 tablespoons plus 2 teaspoons	2/3 cup	
36 teaspoons	12 tablespoons	3/4 cup	6 fluid ounces
42 teaspoons	14 tablespoons	1 cup plus 2 tablespoons	7 fluid ounces
45 teaspoons	15 tablespoons	1 cup minus 1 tablespoon	
48 teaspoons	16 tablespoons	1 cup	8 fluid ounces

Note: Measurement of less than 1/8 teaspoon is considered a dash or a pinch.

INDEX